D0456101

CRITICAL AND CREATIVE THINKING

for teenagers

Carol Carter

Maureen Breeze

LifeBound
DENVER, COLORADO

President/Publisher: Carol J. Carter—LifeBound, LLC
Manager and Training Director: Maureen Breeze
Developmental Editor: Cynthia Nordberg
Managing Editor: Heather Brown
Assistant Editors: Laura Daugherty, Chelsey Emmelhainz, Kristen Fenwick, Kara Kiehle, Natalie Vielkind
Cover & Interior Design: John Wincek, Aerocraft Charter Art Service
Design Interns: Amanda Larghe and Lisabeth Rea
Printing and Binding: Data Reproductions

LifeBound, LLC
1530 High Street
Denver, CO 80218
Tel. 1.877.737.8510
www.lifebound.com

Copyright © 2010 LifeBound, LLC

10 9 8 7 6 5 4 3 2 1

All rights reserved. No part of this publication may be reproduced in any form or by any means, without written permission from the publisher.

Printed in the United States of America.

dedication

To our fathers
who demonstrated tremendous
courage and wherewithal:

John Henry Carter (1916-1991), for his bravery as Captain of the USS Dysson in World War II, his vision for his "great" family, and his love of life.

Gary Allen Breeze (1935-2008), a pilot, banker, rancher, and father, whose will to live inspired all who knew him.

contents

preface

Our goal is to **spark innovative thinking** for your success in the 21st Century. This book is an interactive tool to stoke your imagination and remind you how much there is to learn about the world and your potential contributions to it. Here are the features in the text that promote this expansive thinking:

- Great Thinkers in History
- Great Creators of Today
- Innovations that Changed the World
- Movers & Shakers
- Thinking On the Cutting Edge

The names of some of the inventors and creative thinkers may be obscure, but most of their inventions are not. Through these profiles you'll learn about the fertile minds that gave birth to everything from Listerine mouthwash to Velcro.

The end of chapter activities will help you build skills for the 21st Century. These activities promote deep thinking, team interaction, and the application of technology. Each chapter features one of the world's 20 greatest problems, identified by J.F. Rischard in his groundbreaking book, *High Noon: 20 Global Problems—20 Years to Solve Them*, giving you the opportunity to wrestle with real world problems.

Note: Curriculum for classroom use to accompany this book is available. It includes analytical, creative and practical activities, along with PowerPoint slides and test questions.

We are always looking for ways to improve our student success resources. If you have any ideas about how you or your school could use this book, please send us your thoughts. Here's how to contact us:

Email: contact@lifebound.com

By phone, toll free: 1.877.737.8510

Snail mail: Carol Carter and Maureen Breeze
LifeBound
1530 High St.
Denver, CO 80218

acknowledgments

We extend special thanks to Frank Lyman, Ph.D., Professor Emeritus, University of Maryland, whose life work is devoted to critical and creative thinking for all learners. Dr. Lyman generously shared his expertise with us throughout the revision process of this publication.

We would also like to thank the following people for allowing us to feature them and their work:

Andy Goldsworthy
Diane Lather Belfour
Body Worlds
Susan G. Komen for the Cure, NC Triangle Affiliate
Trace Bundy
Muhammad Yunus
Robert D. Anderson
Craig Newmark
Bimmer Torres and Ratha Sok
Madam C.J. Walker's great-great-granddaughter A'Lelia Bundles
Bill Shore

And we are grateful to the following national and international educators and students who reviewed manuscripts or provided feedback during the development process of *Critical and Creative Thinking for Teenagers:*

Avery Austin, LifeBound coach and National Tutoring Association Board Member

Jenny Beahrs, Director of Design, Teach for America

Sarah Bender, Educational Therapist, Learning Center, Colorado Springs, CO

Carrie Besnette, Metro State College, Denver, CO

Donna Bonatibus, Instructor, Middlesex Community College, Middletown, CT

Barbara S. Bonham, Ph.D., Professor and Coordinator of Higher Education, Appalachian State University

Therese Brown, Dean of Instruction, Front Range Community College, Westminster, CO

Jennifer Burkett, Director of Career Services and External Relations, Carnegie Mellon University

Mirjaliisa Charles, Ph.D., Professor at Helsinki School of Economics, Finland

Becky Cox, Founder and President, Passion for Results, Bloomfield, MI

Alan Craig, Vice President, National College Learning Center Association (NCLCA)

Jim Craven, Principal, Walther Lutheran High School, Melrose Park, IL

Michelle Daugherty, Events Manager, European Council of International Schools (ECIS), London, England

David Daves, Assistant Principal, South High School, Denver CO

Josephine M. I. Diemond, Head of Upper McLean School of Maryland

Jan Friese, Executive director, Texas School Counselor Association

Suzanne Geimer, IB Coordinator, George Washington High School, Denver, CO

Ayesha Hassan, LifeBound coach, Instructor, Circle Learning Center, Charlotte, NC

Mark Heffron, Principal, Denver School of Science and Technology, CO

Rebecca Henderson, Advising Coach, Henderson Community College, Bowling Green, KY

Jane Horn, Principal, Kent Denver School, CO

Carole Hurwitz, Director, Maret Middle School, Washington, DC

Jan Johnson, Associate Executive Director, Summit Preparatory School, Kalispell, MT

Dawn Jones, Director of professional development, DECA

Mary B. Jones, Director of School Leadership, Greeley-Evans School District, CO

Jo Bunton-Keel, Director, Leadership development, Denver Public Schools

Jim Kidder, Director, Center for Teaching International Relations, University of Denver

Michelle Krawchik, Director of Student Achievement, Aurora Public Schools, CO

Mark Lamont, Associate Director of Sales, National Association of Secondary School Principals

Daniel P. Lutz, Ph.D., Principal, Center for International Studies, Denver, CO

Margaret MacLean, International conference presenter and Member of the National School Reform Faculty, Brown University

David E. Malone, Director of Curriculum and Instruction, Colorado Springs District # 11, CO

Debra McKenney, Board Member, Smart-Girl, Denver, CO

Kate Allyn Moore, Senior Editorial Development Manager, Pearson Education

Melinda Morey, M.A., Counselor, Cheyenne Mountain. Junior High School, CO

Carri K. Morgan, Director, Luke Center for Public Service, Punahou School, Honolulu, Hawaii

Deb Mumford, Counselor, West High School, Denver CO

Brian C. Myli, Counselor Specialist, Clark County School District, Las Vegas, NV

Trevor Nordberg, National Honor Society Student, Walther Lutheran High School, Melrose Park, IL

Charlie Nutt, Executive Director, National Academic Advising Association (NACADA)

Linee Perroncel, Denver School of the Arts, CO

Paul Poore, Executive Director, Association of American Schools in South America (AASSA)

Sheila Potoroff, Principal, Conrad Ball Middle School, Ft. Collins, CO

Ryan Rodriguez, Associate Director, Coca Cola Scholars

Jan Romary, Assistant Principal, Golden High School, CO

Christa Roth, Chief Operating Officer, Breakthrough Collaborative

Heidi Moll Schoedel, Team Leader, Odyssey of the Mind, Chicago, IL

Jeff Sherrill, Director of Student Council, National Association of Secondary School Principals

Linda Sills, Associate Director, East Asia Council of Overseas Schools (EARCOS)

Michael Soguero, Director of Professional Development, Eagle Rock School District

Don Stensrud, Principal, Fairview High School, Boulder, CO

Roxanne Lea Taylor, Coordinator of Curriculum Extensions, Park Tudor School, Indianapolis, IN

Lynn Quitman Troyka, Prentice Hall author

Susan C. Wei, Ph.D., High School English Instructional Specialist, Denver Public Schools

Edward Wierzalis, Director of Counseling, University of North Carolina-Charlotte

Antwan Wilson, Assistant Superintendent, Denver Public Schools

Jonathan Wolfer, Principal, Bromwell Elementary School, Denver, CO

Khaki Wonderlich, Instructor, Tomkins Cortland Community College, Dryden, New York

Dr. Kathleen York, Literacy Consultant, Center for Literacy Assessment and Instruction, University of Southern Mississippi

John R. Youngquist, Principal, East High School, Denver, CO

Many thanks to all of you for helping us equip students for school, career and life success in the 21st Century.

Sincerely,

Carol Carter and Maureen Breeze

a special thanks

Our sincere appreciation also goes to Roger Von Oech for his incredible creativity and for granting us permission to cite his Whack Pack Cards throughout the text. At his website, Roger has available a series of products that can take a creative spark and fan it into a raging fire. Go to www.creativethink.com to learn more.

Ask "Why?"
2 Leonardo da Vinci: "I roamed the countryside searching for answers to things I did not understand. Why shells exist on the tops of mountains along with imprints of plants usually found in the sea. Why thunder lasts longer than that which causes it. How circles of water form around the spot which has been struck by a stone. And how a bird suspends itself in the air. Questions like these engaged my thought throughout my life."
What are you curious about? What probing questions can you ask?
1

Creative Whack Pack cards reprinted courtesy of Roger van Oech, © 2007. Visit creativethink.com.

why ask why?

Have you ever witnessed a toddler ask "why," over and over again? Why is the moon round? Why is the sky blue? Why did the flower die? Why does water spill? Why is the stove hot? Perhaps you were such a toddler. This insatiable curiosity helps young children learn about the world around them. The ability to question is the brain's way of making sense, creating order and understanding the world. Unfortunately, our tendency to ask "why" often decreases as we age and mature. The more we are told "what" to think, the less we ask "why."

As a teenager, you've been in school for years. You've learned to read and write, to master formulas and algorithms. So why take time to reflect on how you think? Why try to master strong critical and creative thinking skills?

As you move forward in life, you'll be expected to make responsible decisions for yourself and others. You'll be making choices about your education, about the friends you keep, about your body and your attitudes. You may eventually have children and be responsible for their health and welfare. You'll explore means for supporting yourself and face decisions regarding how to save and invest your money. And in this global market, you'll be competing for jobs with some of the best and brightest people from around the world. In addition, your generation faces serious global challenges, some for which you might be called to participate in the creation of complex solutions.

Yet at the same time, fabulous opportunities await you. Never before have there been as many exciting fields of work to explore, advanced technology to shape communication, and frontiers beyond the earth to conquer. Fifty years ago no one would have ever imagined using DNA to solve crimes or cell phones that take pictures.

An international space station was an idea belonging to science fiction. Yes, today the sky is the limit for those who ask "why," or perhaps, "why not." But you will need well-honed creative and critical thinking skills to participate in such exciting fields.

The purpose of this book is to encourage you as a student and life long learner to never stop asking "why." We'll challenge you to look differently at your own life and the world around you by exploring thinking strategies to help you learn about yourself, improve your problem solving skills, and assist you in making the best decisions possible for your future.

At the same time you will witness great thinking in action. Each chapter introduces a step in the thinking process. We then view the step through a "lens" or thematic concept, so that you learn from real life examples and applications. The lens for this chapter is medicine.

How many of you have been sick and asked why? Why does my throat hurt? Why do I have a fever? Why does my body ache? To answer these questions you might think about whom you've come in contact with or what you've recently eaten.

These "why" questions prompt you to look for a cause, which is at the heart of problem solving. Well-developed critical thinking skills are imperative for exploring such cause and effect relationships. So let's begin by looking at what critical thinking is, and why it's so important.

critical thinking and why it's important

Critical thinking is deeper level thinking. It requires you to go beyond what is simply told to you. It demands that you observe and ask questions; that you analyze problems by looking for cause and effect relationships and comparing and connecting ideas; and that you determine solutions and evaluate outcomes. Critical thinking is analytical and judgmental, helping you work through problems to make decisions.

Here are the basic steps to critical thinking:

1. Asking why—defining why a problem exists
2. Observing the problem
3. Questioning all facets of the situation to gather information
4. Analyzing—recalling what you know; determining cause and effect relationships; and comparing, contrasting and connecting ideas
5. Seeking solutions
6. Evaluating outcomes

To think critically you must also be able to view situations from multiple perspectives. Imagine someone tells you that vaccines are dangerous and that they can cause severe reactions and lead to serious immune disorders. Would you accept this statement as gospel and never agree to have another vaccine? Deeper thinking about such a statement might lead you to consider other perspectives including: where the information about the danger of vaccines came from, what statistics support the statement, what the dangers of not having a vaccine are, and how the risks of a vaccine compare to the dangers of contracting the disease. Thinking about a problem by examining it from many angles will help you make well informed decisions.

Deeper level thinking also involves considering assumptions that might affect the information you're given. For example, what if your doctor suggests you purchase a certain brand of vitamins designed especially for teenagers? If you assume your doctor has your best interests in mind, you might agree to purchase and take the daily vitamins. But what if you discover that your doctor is part owner of this vitamin company and is simply trying to make a profit? How will this information shape your decision?

In sum, critical thinking requires you to reflect on your thought process. It sounds like a lot of work to do what you might believe comes naturally. But this deeper level thinking doesn't come naturally. It takes effort. If you let your thinking become lazy, you'll simply inherit others' ideas for yourself, whether they are positive or negative. You'll make decisions without considering the best possible choices. Without developed critical thinking skills your mind becomes little more than a computer that spits out exactly what it is programmed to do.

Imagine a computer that has been programmed to solve complex mathematic equations one day stops mid-stream and announces it has a far more efficient means of problem solving. This scenario could never happen. A computer can not "re-think" a strategy. A computer merely processes information according to how it's programmed. But you can. This is the difference between your mind and a computer, and a significant reason why you'll benefit from honing your critical thinking skills.

how are your critical thinking skills?

Let's stop here to reflect on your current critical thinking skills. Answer these questions as they relate to various areas in your life *(i.e. a problem with a friend, a science experiment, a failed audition for the school play, etc.)*.

1. I ask why a problem exists before I try to solve it.

ALWAYS	USUALLY	SELDOM	NEVER

Describe a time when you asked why a problem existed before attempting to solve it, and as a result had an easier time coming up with a solution.

____

____

____

2. I am a careful observer.

ALWAYS	USUALLY	SELDOM	NEVER

When have you carefully observed your surroundings and it paid off for you?

____

____

____

3. I generate a list of questions about the problem before trying to solve it.

ALWAYS	USUALLY	SELDOM	NEVER

Describe a time when you asked a lot of questions before solving a problem. How did the answers to the questions help you?

____

____

____

4. I analyze a problem by looking for a cause and effect relationship before I implement a solution.

ALWAYS	USUALLY	SELDOM	NEVER

When have you failed to look for a cause and effect relationship in a situation before you took action? In other words, when have you reacted spontaneously to a problem without thinking about the cause of it, and your response backfired?

5. I compare, contrast and connect ideas about a problem before I decide how to solve it.

ALWAYS	USUALLY	SELDOM	NEVER

Describe a time when you've compared, contrasted and connected ideas about a problem and as a result, generated an excellent solution.

6. I take time to evaluate the outcomes of my decisions or solutions to problems.

ALWAYS	USUALLY	SELDOM	NEVER

Write about a time where you made a decision or solved a problem in an unsatisfactory manner. What did you learn by evaluating the outcome of your solution?

7. I memorize material for tests and soon forget the information once the class is completed.

ALWAYS	USUALLY	SELDOM	NEVER

When have you learned something, forgotten it, and then needed the information, wishing you'd mastered it rather than memorized it for short term?

How did you do? If you're like most teenagers, you have some answers demonstrating active critical thinking and others revealing opportunities for improvement.

One of the best ways to learn about deeper level thinking is to see it in action. To accomplish this, we've included a profile of a great thinker from history in each chapter to demonstrate the concepts being discussed. In this chapter we highlight Florence Nightingale, a nurse from the 1800's who dared to ask "why" in an era where women were not encouraged to challenge conventional thought, and were more likely to take orders than lead directives.

Florence Nightingale 1820–1910

Have you heard of Florence Nightingale? If so, what comes to mind when you hear her name? When most people think of Florence Nightingale, they envision a nurse sitting bedside, patiently tending to the sick. However, her contributions had more to do with mathematics than nursing.

Florence Nightingale was born in Florence, Italy and received a broad education in Greek, Italian and History. She was passionate

about mathematics, but it was not proper for young women at that time to study the subject. After years of pleading with her parents, they finally conceded and she became well schooled in mathematics and statistics. She then became a nurse and worked for the British government during the Crimean War.

In 1854, while stationed at a British war camp, she saw thousands of soldiers die in her hospital. They weren't dying from the wounds themselves, but from infections contracted while being treated for their wounds.

If you were Florence Nightingale what "why" questions might you ask?

Miss Nightingale asked:

- Why are more soldiers dying in this hospital than on the battle field?
- What conditions exist in the hospital that might be contributing to the deaths of the soldiers?
- Why is no one letting fresh air into the hospital rooms?
- Why are patients sleeping on the dirty floors?

By stopping to ask why, she developed questions that shaped her understanding. She used her math skills to compile important statistics and came to the conclusion, which was radical at the time, that poor patient hygiene and lack of sanitary conditions contributed to soldiers dying from infection ten times more often than from battle wounds. Because the number of soldiers available to fight the war was beginning to dwindle due to the large number of fatalities resulting from infections, she had to convince the government that changes must be made in the hospitals.

TRYING IT OUT . . .

Imagine you were Florence Nightingale, working at a hospital that treats soldiers during a war. You've gathered the following statistics revealing the number of deaths and their causes in your hospital.

	April	May	June	July	Aug	Sept	Oct	Nov	Dec	Jan	Feb	Mar
Deaths from wounds	0	0	0	0	0	52	80	107	90	49	30	29
Deaths from infections	0	5	4	180	260	250	170	270	310	360	330	300
Deaths from other causes	20	18	5	25	26	5	3	2	8	40	60	40

Find a partner and work together to create a graph or visual representation of the numbers that will help teach others about the problem and what needs to be done to fix it.

Miss Nightingale needed to present such statistics to the authorities to convince them to make changes in hospital care. She wanted to capture their attention with a powerful visual aid, so she created revolutionary pie charts, now known as coxcomb graphs. With her creative visual aids, she was able to convince the British government that if they continued to have soldiers needlessly die from infections at the current rate, they'd soon run out of soldiers to fight the war.

On the following page is a coxcomb graph that Florence Nightingale created from her statistics.

Florence Nightingale questioned "why" and had the critical thinking skills to then determine the causes of the problem. As a result, she was able to convince the government to change hospital procedures and the mortality rate of the British soldiers decreased significantly. In fact, many of the hygiene and sanitation practices we consider standard in hospitals today result from her asking "why" over one hundred and fifty years ago. This profile illustrates how one woman's ability to use critical thinking skills and express her knowledge in a creative way has changed the world we live in today.

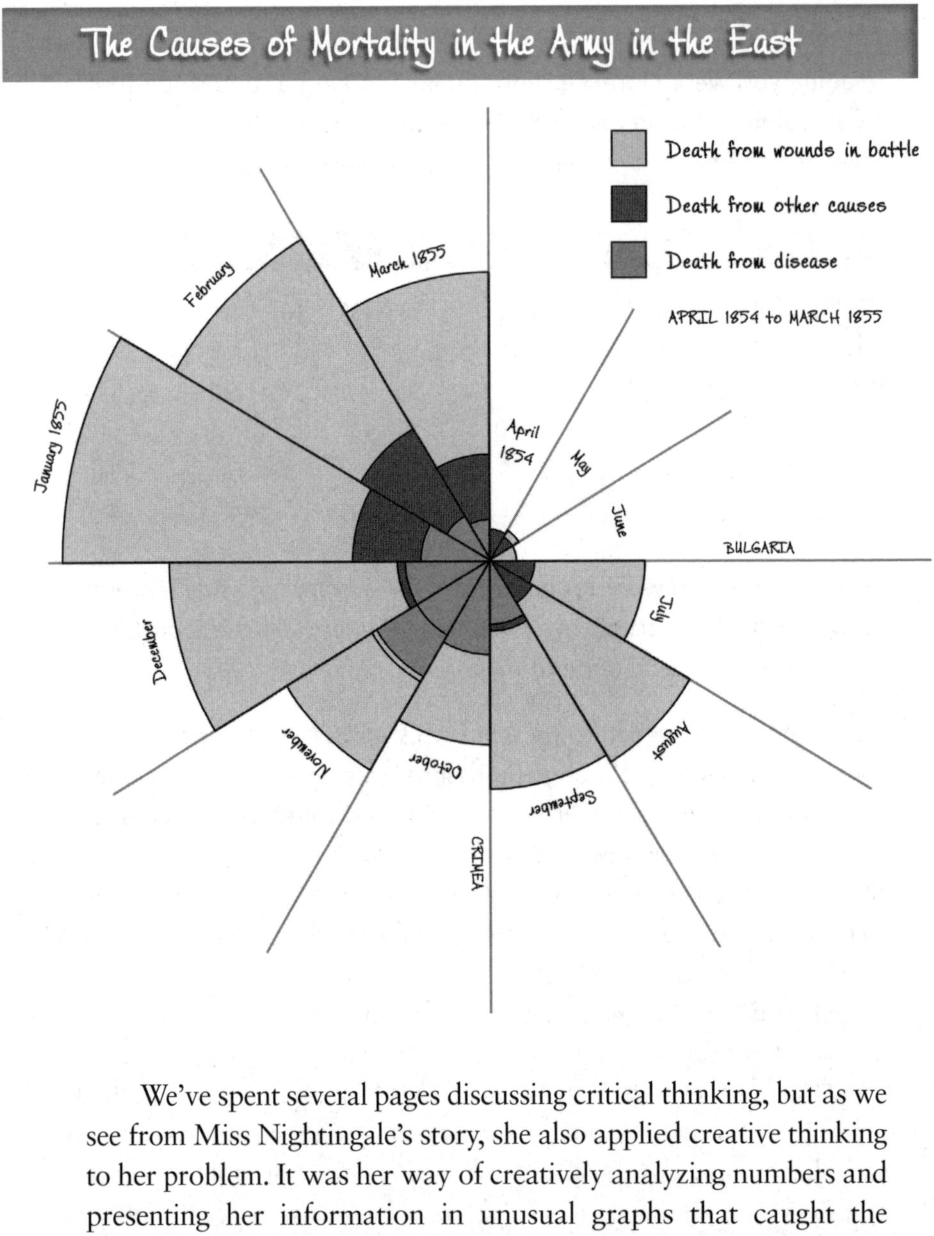

We've spent several pages discussing critical thinking, but as we see from Miss Nightingale's story, she also applied creative thinking to her problem. It was her way of creatively analyzing numbers and presenting her information in unusual graphs that caught the authorities' attention and convinced them to follow her suggestions.

Problem solving often requires both critical and creative thinking, yet there are conceptual differences in these thought processes. So let's take a moment to examine creative thinking and consider how it differs from critical thinking.

creative thinking and why it is important

Creativity is the ability to produce and express original ideas. It involves using your imagination to bring about something new and unique, whether it is a physical structure, a fresh perspective, or a piece of art. While critical thinking is analytical and selective, directed at formulating a specific solution to a problem, creative thinking is generative and expansive, aimed at producing novel outcomes.

Creative thinking has been analyzed and written about for ages, but is commonly described as a process that includes the following steps:

1. Asking why a problem exists
2. Observing the problem
3. Reflecting on what you know
4. Letting go of what you know to gain new perspectives
5. Brainstorming fresh ideas
6. Testing new ideas
7. Evaluating ideas as possible solutions

Try solving the following riddle using the steps for creative thinking. *(Hint: Remember this is a riddle, not a traditional math problem)*

13 + 5 = 0	31+8 = 2	16 + 2 = ?
20 + 6 = 2	81+6 = 3	68 + 1 = ?
11 + 3 = 0	10+0 = 2	90 + 6 = ?

Any luck? If not, don't feel bad. This riddle was given to both kindergartners and college students to answer. And the surprising result—kindergarteners had greater success than college students at correctly solving it.

Perhaps their success stems from not having the idea reinforced for many years that according to the addition principle, 13 + 5 = 18, and 20 + 6 = 26. By not being stuck in this one line of thinking, they are free to explore other possible patterns and connections.

Look again at the riddle. Do you see any other patterns emerge which aren't related to the addition principle? Consider the shapes of each number.

If you ask yourself why 13 + 5 = 0, yet 90 + 6 = 3, and view the numbers as drawn shapes instead of numeric values, you'll see that 13 + 5 has no shapes with a closed loop, and its answer is zero. However, 90 + 6 has three shapes with closed loops. The 9, 0 and 6 each have one, and as a result, its answer is 3.

Let's go back to our riddle and explore creative thinking in this context.

1. **What is the problem?** A series of equations to be solved where the left side of the equal sign is equivalent, in some manner, to the right side of the equation.
2. **What do you know about the problem?** The two sides of the equation should be equal. It doesn't follow what we know about addition of numeric values.
3. **What do you need to let go of to achieve new perspectives?** We must suspend our knowledge of numeric addition.
4. **What new ideas can you apply to the problem?** Here we brainstorm possible solutions—perhaps the number of the actual digits on the left will equal the right; maybe the number on the right reflects how many even or odd numbers are on the left side of the equation; the number of closed loops drawn on the left side of the equation equals the number on the right side; etc. This is the step where we generate ideas.
5. **How might your ideas solve the problem?** By testing the generated solutions in step 4, we see that only the final idea—the number of loops drawn on the left side equals the number on the right side—works as a solution.

6. **How does your idea hold up as an effective solution to the problem?** This final step calls for you to verify your solution against the problem over and over again. So here, you go back through each equation and verify that your solution holds in each instance.

By being able to ask yourself why the relationships in the riddle exist, and consider the problem from another perspective, you are exercising your creative thinking skills. Many define creative thinking as a process that generates art, which it indeed does. But as you've just seen, creative thinking can be used to solve all types of problems.

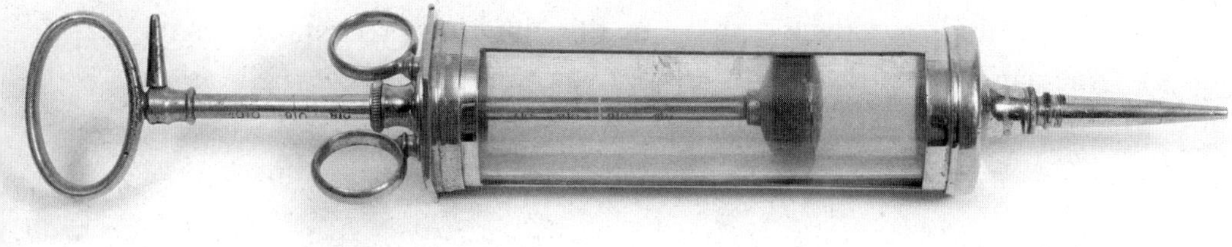

Alexander Wood and Charles Gabriel Pravez created the first hypodermic syringe with a hollow pointed needle for intravenous injections and infusions, 1853.

how creative are you?

Let's stop to reflect on your creative thinking skills.

_____ How many times a day do you try something new?

_____ Do you like to take risks with new ideas?

_____ What creative activities are you involved with on a regular basis?

_____ How often do you tend to do things the same way you always do, just because it is comfortable?

_____ Do you like to solve problems, riddles and magic tricks?

_____ Do you ever play the devil's advocate (taking a different point of view from the members in a group)?

_____ What is the greatest creative project you've ever been involved with?

_____ Do you like thinking creatively?

With the above answers in mind, rate your creativity on the scale below (1 being low, 10 being high).

1	2	3	4	5	6	7	8	9	10

Whether you rated your creative abilities as low or high, there is room for all of us to grow in this area. You can always try something new, add a twist to your approach, or look at a problem from an unusual angle. That is the beauty of creative thinking. And by learning to actively engage in this thinking process, you may one day be responsible for an innovation that changes the world.

INNOVATIONS
CHANGING THE WORLD

How many of you have had a doctor, nurse or dentist wear rubber gloves while treating you? Have you witnessed doctors scrubbing their hands, wearing face masks or using sterilized instruments during medical procedures? These practices resulted from the creative insights of Dr. Josef Lister whose ideas radically changed the way medical practitioners work today.

Joseph Lister (1821-1912) was a doctor from England. During his time, nearly fifty percent of all patients died from infection after having surgery. Can you imagine going in to a hospital to have your tonsils removed, knowing that there was only a fifty percent chance of coming home alive? Dr. Lister was one of the first physicians to stop and analyze why so many people died after surgery.

If you were Dr. Lister, what "why" questions would you ask?

____

____

____

During this era, infection was believed to transfer through the air. As a result, doctors didn't feel it was necessary to wash their hands and sterilize their equipment when working with patients. However, Dr. Lister suspected otherwise. Ignoring the commonly held belief at the time that germs could not spread from a doctor's skin to a patient's wounds, he set out to create methods for sterilizing hands and medical instruments that would kill microorganisms that just might be causing infection. To do this, he used a chemical solution of carbolic acid to dress wounds. He also demanded that all the nurses and doctors working with him scrub their hands and instruments with this chemical solution.

These were radical steps one hundred and fifty years ago. When several of the nurses complained that the carbolic acid solution was hurting their skin, he asked Charles Goodyear, the rubber making giant, to make gloves for them to wear when treating patients. And this is how the rubber glove made its way into the practice of medicine.

Can you imagine cutting your chin open and having a doctor stitch you without wearing rubber gloves or washing his or her hands? We can all thank Dr. Lister for his creative, revolutionary ideas. And how many of you have heard of Listerine mouthwash? This product also uses a chemical solution that kills microorganisms living in people's mouths; thereby alleviating bad breath. It was named in honor of Dr. Lister and his creative thinking which revolutionized the way germs are handled today.

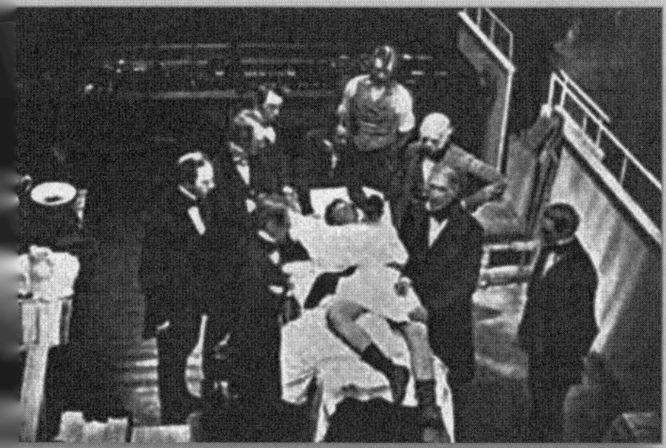

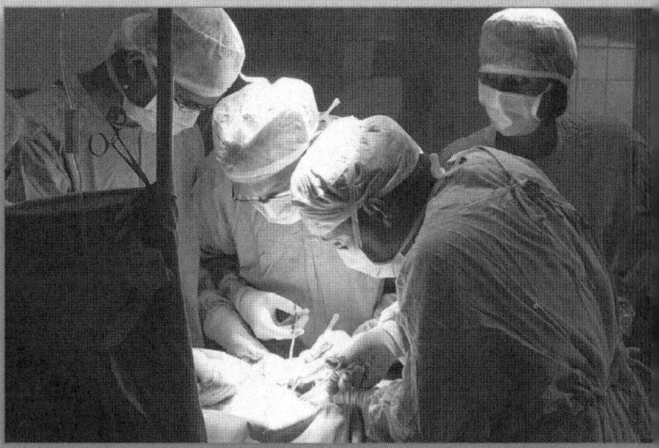

As these examples demonstrate, the field of medicine has benefited from both creative and critical thinking. The two go hand in hand. Both Lister and Nightingale employed critical thinking strategies to define the problems, to look for cause and effect relationships, and to analyze what they knew by comparing, contrasting and connecting ideas. At the same time, they suspended their thinking about the common beliefs of the time (that sanitary conditions weren't related to the spread of infection and that germs couldn't be transferred by human contact), and expanded their thinking to create new approaches to the problem. As you'll see throughout this book, critical and creative thinking complement one another, allowing you to approach problems from multiple angles.

Whenever you face a problem, whether you are approaching it with critical thinking to analyze and formulate a specific solution, or with creative thinking to generate a unique response to a problem, you can follow our thinking road map. Chapters 1–6 are dedicated to each of these steps on the map, and discuss both the critical and creative thinking involved with each of these actions.

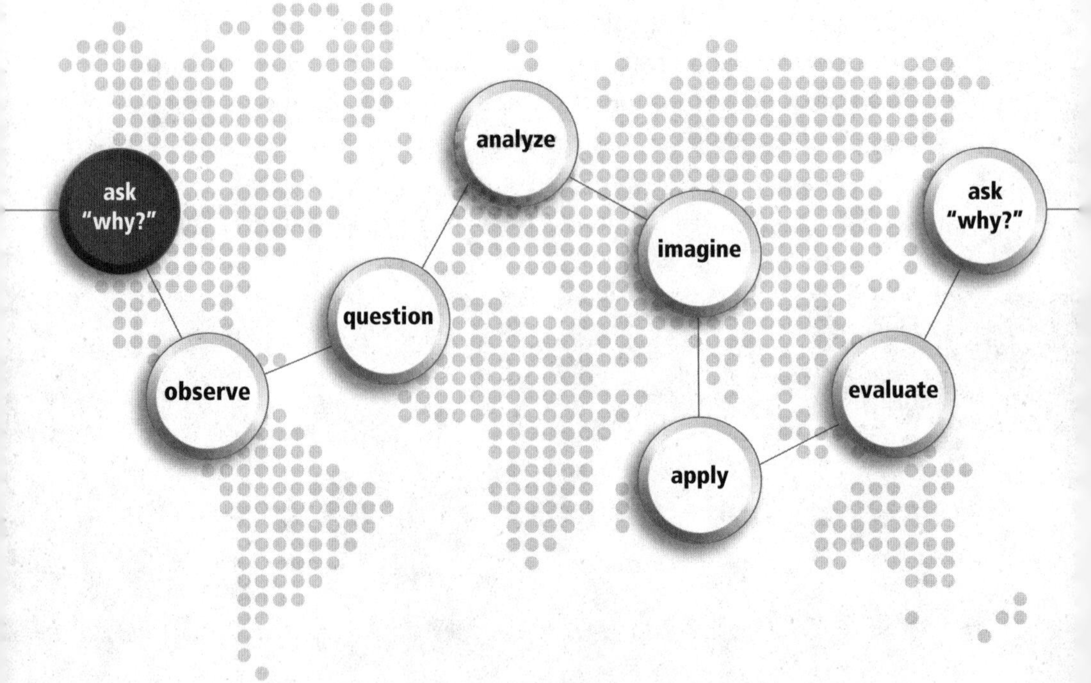

Take a moment to reflect: How does Miss Nightingale's mathematic analysis and Mr. Lister's use of carbolic acid demonstrate both creative and critical thinking?

how do critical and creative thinking relate to your life?

If you end up in a hospital or need to have surgery you can thank Florence Nightingale or Joseph Lister for "asking why!" But how does this deeper thinking relate to you, a high school student? You might not believe you can change the world today by asking why. However, the people profiled in this chapter were successful in doing this, and changed the world as a result, because they learned to ask why early in their lives.

As a teen, Florence Nightingale wasn't allowed to study math. But she asked why over and over again, persisting until her father finally agreed. She also questioned her parents when they wouldn't approve of her working as a nurse, as it was uncommon for wealthy women to work in her day. She developed a habit of challenging conventional thought and asking why early in her life—just as you can today.

Where in your life can you ask why? Why are you in school? Why do you have the friends you do? Why are you enrolled in the classes you're currently taking? If it is assumed you'll go into your family's business after graduation, have you asked why? If your teachers think you'll never succeed in college, have you asked why? This is your first step to critical and creative thinking. Now is the time to ask why.

This book will give you many opportunities to ask questions, to challenge assumptions, to practice analyzing information and to deepen your learning. By committing to the reading and completing the activities, you will develop the thinking skills needed in the 21st century. In a world constantly changing with new technology, employers value strong thinking skills above all else, and these will be your best tools for work place success. Mastering these abilities in high school will offer you more options for college and will help you secure the best jobs once you enter the world of work.

If you decide you don't want to work for a traditional company, you can use your creative and critical thinking skills to develop the next iPod, a show on Comedy Central, the best selling fuel efficient car, or perhaps the cure for cancer. Whatever your ambitions, mastering your thinking will help you achieve your personal and professional dreams.

POWERFUL QUESTIONS FOR DISCUSSION

1. Is medicine a science that emphasizes critical thinking, or an art emphasizing creative thinking?
2. Choose another recent advancement in medicine that is changing how we understand and deal with both disease and health. How have creative and critical thinking strategies been applied to reach this advancement?
3. When in history have groups of humans been discouraged to "ask why" regarding their own health? What were the forces at play that discouraged deeper level thinking?
4. When do you resist deeper level thinking regarding your own health and well being? What might it cost you?

BUILDING SKILLS
FOR THE TWENTY-FIRST CENTURY

Challenging Your Thinking

ASKING WHY

Answer the following questions and add three reasons why you've given your response.

What is your favorite thing to do after school?

____

Now ask yourself why.

1. ____
2. ____
3. ____

Who do you like to spend time with?

____

Now ask yourself why.

1. ____
2. ____
3. ____

What is your hardest class?

____

Now ask yourself why.

1. ____
2. ____
3. ____

What is your favorite subject to study?

____

Now ask yourself why.

1. ______________________________
2. ______________________________
3. ______________________________

What is your favorite holiday?

____

Now ask yourself why.

1. ______________________________
2. ______________________________
3. ______________________________

Who is the most challenging person to get along with that you know?

____

Now ask yourself why.

1. ______________________________
2. ______________________________
3. ______________________________

What is your greatest hope for the future?

____

Now ask yourself why.

1. ______________________________
2. ______________________________
3. ______________________________

What causes anxiety in your life?

____

Now ask yourself why.

1. ______________________________
2. ______________________________
3. ______________________________

What is your best personal habit?

____

Now ask yourself why.

1. ______________________________
2. ______________________________
3. ______________________________

What was your most recent failure?

____

Now ask yourself why.

1. ______________________________
2. ______________________________
3. ______________________________

What do you like about your family?

____

Now ask yourself why.

1. ______________________________
2. ______________________________
3. ______________________________

What would you like to change about your life?

____

Now ask yourself why.

1. ______________________________
2. ______________________________
3. ______________________________

How has "asking why" in this activity informed you about yourself?

Practicing What You Learned

THE SUPER BUG

Despite all we've learned about germs and how to prevent their spreading, new issues continue to arrive demanding critical and creative thinking skills. How many of you have heard of the Super Bug?

The Super Bug, officially known as methicillin-resistant staphylococcus aureus, or MRSA, consists of bacteria often found on the skin and in the noses of healthy people. It generally causes no problems. But the elderly and very young, along with those who have run down immune systems, are susceptible to becoming ill from these microorganisms. MRSA was first detected in 1961 but has spread and become a more common problem, most often affecting people in hospitals and other health care related settings. Unfortunately, because the bacteria are resistant to most antibiotics, the super bug can be deadly. It now strikes as many as 90,000 people a year. According to a public health expert quoted on an ABC News Report on October 17, 2007, deaths tied to these infections may soon exceed those caused by AIDS.

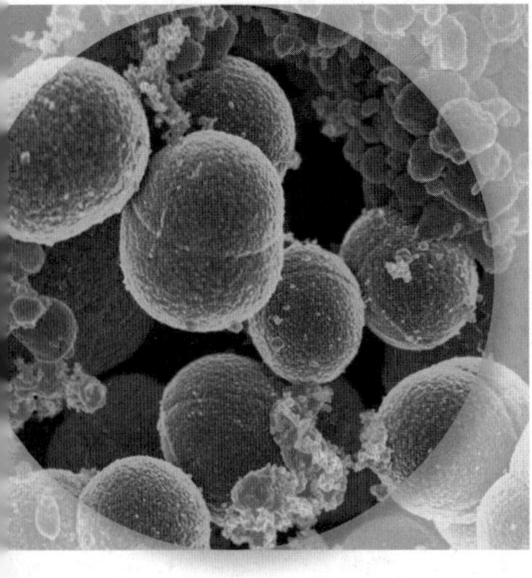

If you were a doctor trying to stop the spread of the Super Bug, what "why" questions would you ask:

____

____

____

____

____

Putting Your Heads Together

SOLVING THE WORLD'S GREATEST PROBLEMS

Global infectious diseases. One of the most challenging issues facing the world today is the spread of global infectious diseases.

Imagine you and your classmates are asked by the World Health Organization to join a committee addressing this difficult issue.

Divide into smaller teams and complete the following:

- Research the most prominent global infectious diseases of modern day.
- Choose one and think about why this disease poses a threat.
- Examine why and how it spreads.
- Think about the consequences of an international breakout of your chosen disease.
- Generate three ideas to help minimize the spreading of the disease and suggestions for how you might implement these solutions.
- Present your findings and share your recommendations to the class.

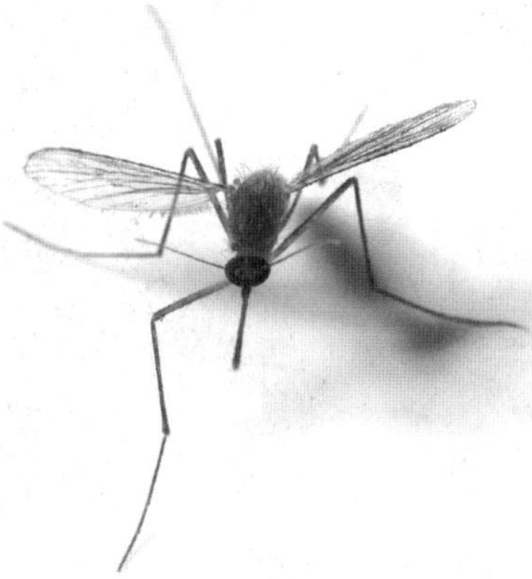

Get out of Your Box

3 Each culture has its own way of looking at the world. Often the best ideas come from cutting across disciplinary boundaries and looking into other fields. As Bob Wieder put it, "Anyone can look for fashion in a boutique or history in a museum. The creative explorer looks for history in a hardware store and fashion in an airport." Example: World War I military designers borrowed from the Cubist art of Picasso to create more efficient camouflage patterns for tanks. **In what outside places can you look for ideas?**

Creative Whack Pack cards reprinted courtesy of Roger van Oech, © 2007. Visit creativethink.com.

how to observe

Once you've identified the problem at hand, you can begin to think about how to solve it. Florence Nightingale asked herself why so many soldiers were dying in the hospital. From this question she identified the problem that more soldiers in the hospital were dying from infection than from war wounds. Only then did she begin solving the problem by observing all she could about the infections the soldiers were contracting in the hospital.

Taking the time to observe the situation before acting is critical. Let's look at an example you can relate to.

Imagine you are hiking alone in the mountains. You've climbed for hours and decide it's time to make your way back down the mountain. As you descend down the trail, you meet a fork in the path. Suddenly you don't know whether to go right or left. By asking yourself why it matters which way you go, you realize that it's getting dark and you will be lost if you take the wrong turn. You've identified a problem. Would you quickly choose one path over the other, without thinking it through? Probably not. The first thing you'd most likely do is stop and observe your surroundings. You might con-

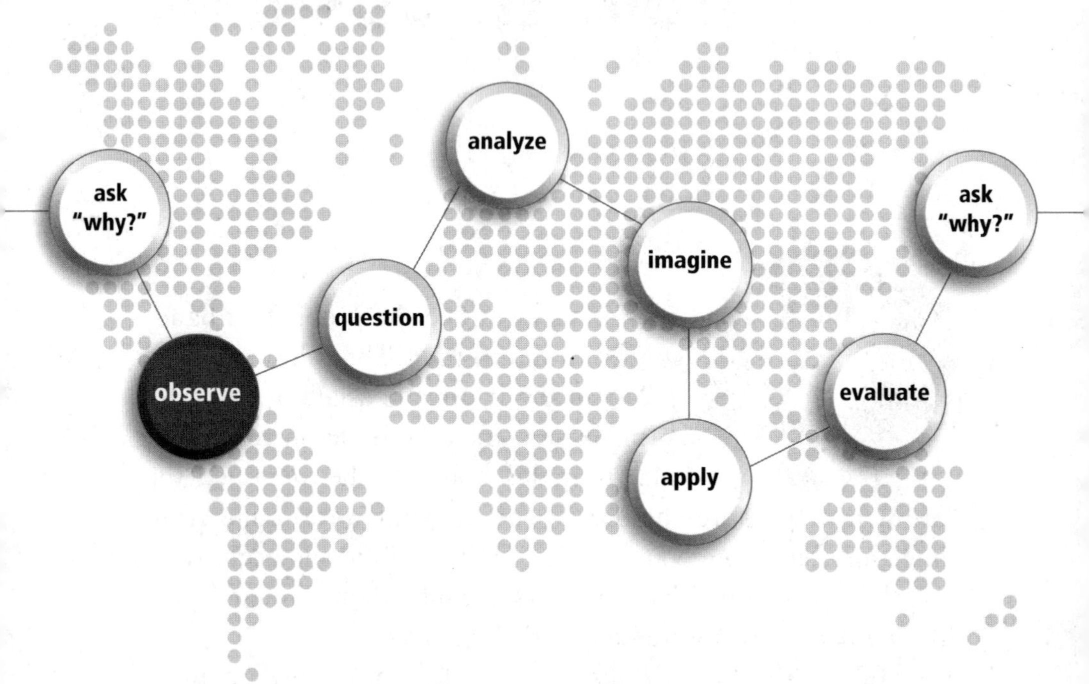

sider whether anything looks familiar. Or perhaps you'd observe where the sun is and connect this with where it was positioned while you were climbing up the hill. Or maybe you'd listen to where the sounds of a stream are coming from to find your bearings. The point is that you must take time to observe before you react.

Think of a firefighter stepping into a flaming building not knowing where the fire is burning. Would it make the most sense for him to run into the first room he comes upon and spray water from the hose? Absolutely not! A better strategy would be for the fireman to quickly observe the fire: to use his eyes to see where the fire is burning, to use his sense of smell to detect smoke, to use his sense of hearing to listen for floors collapsing or voices of people calling for help, and finally to use his sense of feeling to detect where heat intensifies in the building. By using all his senses to gather the most information possible, he's better prepared to fight the fire.

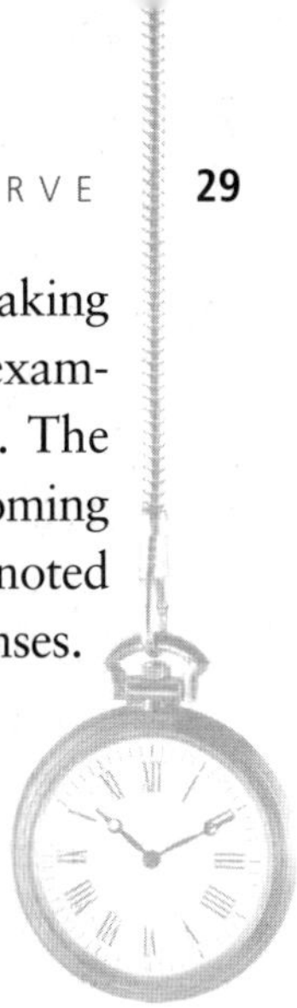

As you can see, investing time to observe is critical for making the best decisions, even in emergency situations. But as the examples above illustrate, observing does not just mean seeing. The Merriam-Webster dictionary defines the word observe as "coming to realize or know especially through the consideration of noted facts." And these noted facts are gathered through all the senses.

take a moment to reflect

List five 21st century occupations that require effective observation skills:

1. ______________________________
2. ______________________________
3. ______________________________
4. ______________________________
5. ______________________________

Here are some jobs that you may not have considered:

Continuity script supervisor. Do you know that scenes from movies are rarely filmed in chronological order? As a result, there can be inconsistencies with the costumes and sets when the film is put together and edited. For example, an actor may wear a watch one day when filming a scene, but he may forget the watch two weeks later when filming a consecutive scene. When the editors finally paste the scenes together, the actor's costume is inconsistent. To handle such issues, directors rely on a script supervisor to observe each scene before it is filmed to make sure all the elements such as costumes, props and lighting are consistent from one day to the next.

Professional tasters. How would you like to get paid to taste chocolate? To eat steak? To sample coffee? Professional eaters are trained to taste food for quality and con-

sistency before it lands on the shelves of grocery stores or on the menus of restaurants. Professional eaters are trained to use their noses along with their mouths because as much as 80% of taste is related to smell. Centers for research such as Chapman University's Sensory Evaluation Laboratory in California trains professionals to develop the sensory skills to effectively evaluate a variety of food products. Professional eaters can make anywhere from $30,000 a year, to senior executive salaries of over $100,000 a year.

Massage therapists for horses. Many professional equestrians turn to massage therapy for their horses. Research shows massage and therapeutic touch can help relieve chronic pain, stimulate circulation and increase horses' flexibility. Because these animals can't easily communicate their needs and areas of physical pain, it takes a highly sensitive massage therapist to accurately treat them. As a result, the therapists with the greatest observation skills are in high demand. There are several accredited massage therapy schools today that specialize in training therapists to treat animals.

how to develop your observation skills

Whether you want to pursue one of the careers mentioned above, or you want to simply improve your critical and creative thinking, enhancing your observational skills will only help you. Yet developing these abilities requires both practice and patience: practice, because you need to do it over and over each day to turn this step of thinking into a habit, and patience because you need to slow yourself down when faced with a problem to observe how your senses respond to the situation.

Imagine your friend approaches you and says she needs help. Before you even ask what she needs, you can use your observation skills to assess the situation. Her words tell you she needs help. What else do you get from hearing the tone of her voice—is she anxious, hurried, or relaxed? You see her move toward you. But what else do you see? Does she have a frown on her face, appear out of breath, or look at ease? Is she running or walking? What else does her body language suggest? Do you smell anything else that might suggest trouble? Does she grab your arm when asking for help or does she stand several feet away?

By taking time to observe the context of how this one sentence of information is being delivered, you learn a lot about the seriousness of the problem and how you might best respond.

So when you observe a problem, go through a quick check list and ask:

- What do I see?
- What do I hear?
- What do I smell?
- What do I taste?
- What do I feel?
- What is my intuition, or gut, telling me?

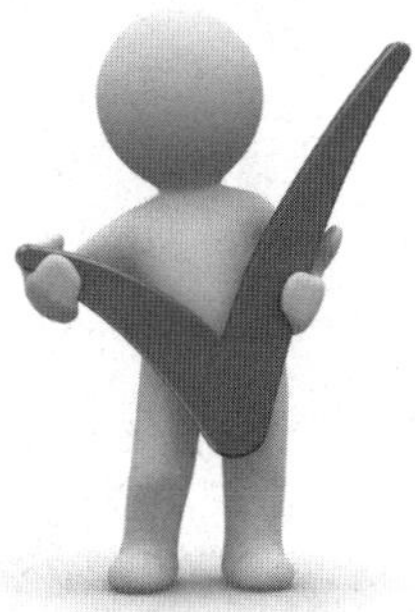

In addition to asking yourself these questions, take note of how your body physically reacts when you face a situation. Does your heart start racing, do your shoulders drop with relief, or does your stomach churn with anxiety? Often, your internal reactions provide insightful information.

It might feel as if this is a lot to do every time you face a problem. But with practice, this process will become second nature. And in time you'll learn quickly to pick up on nuances and details that will help you solve problems in your personal life, in school and eventually, in your career, preparing you to succeed in the 21st century.

Let's stop for a moment and assess your observation skills.

how observant are you?

1. Which sense do you rely on the most? The least?

____

____

____

2. Can you remember the eye color of three of your classmates?

____

____

____

3. When you enter a room full of strangers, what do you notice?

____

____

____

4. Describe a time when you failed to fully observe a situation or problem. What happened? What did it cost you?

____

____

____

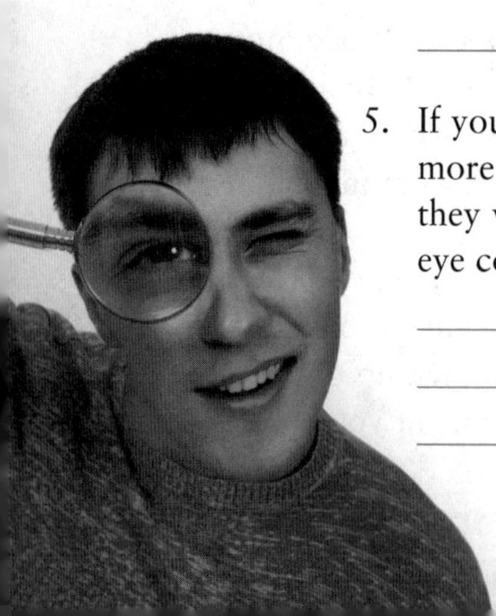

5. If you meet someone for the first time are you more likely to remember their name, the clothes they wear, their handshake, their scent or their eye color?

____

____

____

6. Do you keep a journal? If so, what captures your attention enough to be remembered and recorded?

7. Describe a situation you have observed that triggered a "gut" reaction.

8. Who has the best observation skills you know? What advantages do they have because of these skills?

9. On a scale from 1–10, 1 being the low and 10 being the high, rate your observation skills. Which sense is the most difficult for you to use for observing?

1	2	3	4	5	6	7	8	9	10

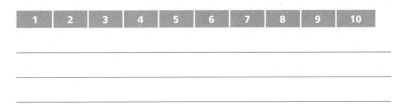

By putting yourself in new situations and making a conscious effort to observe all you can, you'll begin to fine tune these skills. A fun example of this type of practice is The New York Police Academy which has trained many of its officers by sending them to art museums to study various paintings. By asking the officers to stop and really see the paintings, they heightened their abilities to see, observe and sense their world around them and as a result, improved their performance on the job. Similarly, the Yale School of Medicine has used visual art and creative writing exercises to help its students make quick and astute observations in a variety of situations, which is a skill all physicians need.

Describe one thing you'll do throughout this next week to improve your observation abilities.

Throughout this chapter we are going to examine how we observe using examples from nature. Because of the way nature shifts, changes and evolves, it provides a fascinating canvas for observation. Try the following activity that calls for you to use your imagination to set a stage in nature where you can practice your observation skills.

imagining observations

Pretend you are standing alone in a thick forest at dusk. Take three minutes to imagine your surroundings. Create details in your mind, being as specific as possible. Don't forget to consider all of your senses. After you have time to envision a vivid picture of your surroundings, write down your observations below.

What did you see? (Go beyond listing a tree. Describe what kind of tree, what is at your feet, how much light hits the top branches, etc. Try to generate as many details as possible.)

What did you hear? (Did you hear close range noise, background noise, voices in your head, etc.?)

____

____

____

What did you smell? (Were smells coming from the air, from the ground, on your fingertips, etc.?)

____

____

____

What did you feel? (You can address both physical and emotional feelings—rain falling on your skin, wind blowing through your hair, your heart racing, etc.)

____

____

____

What did your instincts tell you? (Did you feel safe, in danger, near others, lost, etc.?)

____

____

____

This activity is a great way to practice observing details. And taking note of them can help you make quick decisions if something suddenly happens. What if a bear came from around a tree? What if you suddenly heard a stranger calling out your name? By being observant and taking note of your surroundings, you are better prepared to respond effectively.

how powerful observation skills benefit you

Being a careful observer will not only help in a crisis situation, but will benefit you in other ways as well.

By being a skillful observer, you'll be a better student because you can:

1. listen to follow directions more accurately
2. see the full scope of problems/assignments
3. interpret what teachers emphasize as the most important information
4. identify helpful resources that relate to the problems you face

By being a skillful observer, you'll be a better communicator because you can:

1. read body language
2. hear the tone of someone's voice
3. view the context the message is delivered in
4. sense/interpret the motivation of the speaker

By being a skillful observer, you'll be safer because you can:

1. take note of your surroundings
2. assess potential danger areas
3. witness peoples' actions and behaviors that may be cause for danger
4. respond to your intuition or "gut" feelings that warn you of trouble

By being a skillful observer, you'll be a better friend because you can:

1. sense when someone's in need
2. know when you need the support of others

3. see when relationships change and observe what might be triggering such change
4. pick up on the dynamics that positively and negatively affect your friendships

The ability to observe is a life skill which can help you become a powerful critical and creative thinker. Our Great Creator of Today for this chapter is an artist who has relied upon this skill above all others in his career. By placing himself in nature and observing his surroundings, Andy Goldsworthy has developed award winning sculptures, using only the surrounding nature for his art.

GREAT CREATORS OF TODAY

Andy Goldsworthy

British artist Andy Goldsworthy is best known for the site-specific sculptures that he creates in collaboration with nature. He has crafted masterpieces around the world, involving only the natural elements he has at his fingertips, whether it is reeds, thorns, rocks or ice. If it is snowing, he works with snow. If leaves are falling, he works with leaves.

It is his keen power of observation, of seeing the potential in what nature presents to him on any given day, which helps him create such magical art. Because his work lives and dies with the cycles of nature, it is often difficult to capture for the world to see. However a beautiful documentary, Rivers and Tides, showcases some of his work and is available in most public libraries.

observing our world

Observing nature, for both aesthetic and survival purposes, is something humans have done since the beginning of time. Man's survival has depended on the ability to observe animal migration habits, weather patterns, and the effect seasons have on our access to food and water. And as a result, we've learned as a species to live hand in hand with nature. However, new observations are radically changing how we view and care for our planet.

Recently, scientists have been noticing radical changes on earth. Their observations include melting ice caps, rising temperatures, shifts in weather patterns and rising sea levels—all pointing to global climate change. These collective observations are being acknowledged and global climate change is now recognized as a serious world problem demanding attention.

Former Vice President Al Gore has worked to raise awareness of the observations scientists have been making. His film, *An Inconvenient Truth*, shows us how our dependency on fossil fuels and other types of energy adversely affect nature. His efforts have triggered responses to the difficult problems that lie ahead. Innovations stemming from such observations are now gaining ground. Consider the work of Isaac Berzin.

INNOVATIONS
CHANGING THE WORLD

Isaac Berzin, *Founder of GreenFuel Technologies*

Isaac Berzin is a chemical engineer who was raised and educated in Israel. He is reinventing the energy business by discovering natural processes to develop renewable fuels. He recently signed a $92 million contract to grow what most people scrape out of their fish tanks: algae. This unusual crop may one day provide a way out of our dependency on fossil fuels and the environmental destruction they're causing.

By taking the time to observe the properties of algae, Isaac discovered they double their mass in a few hours, produce thirty times more oil per acre as sunflowers do, and thrive in sewage, or brackish water. He also observed that single-cell algae consume carbon dioxide and other troubling power plant emissions, and, even better, they emit oxygen during photosynthesis. This makes single-cell algae tiny power plants in their own right—power plants that may transform toxic emissions to renewable energy.

Isaac's idea is simple once you understand algae's appetites and its astonishing efficiency. Laboratory research at GreenFuel has already demonstrated that single-cell algae could consume carbon dioxide or nitrogen oxides and then be "harvested" in a reusable form. This form, a biomass, could potentially be burned like coal, liquefied into oil, or used to make plastics, nutraceuticals or food. Berzin's observations may one day change energy production throughout the world.

Sources: http://web.mit.edu/newsoffice/2004/algae.html, http://www.time.com/time/specials/2007/article/0,28804,1733748_1733754_1735703,00.html

Matt Mathis, left, and Roger Simmons, technicians with the Center of Excellence for Hazardous Materials Management, sample the water in a stock tank being used to grow algae at New Mexico State University's Agricultural Science Center at Artesia. Researchers are working to determine the best methods to grow and harvest the algae, which can be used to produce oil for bio-diesel fuel.

Photo by Darrell J. Pehr, http://ucommphoto.nmsu.edu/newsphoto/algae_biodiesel.jpg.

when you fail to observe

By observing the problems with our current energy sources, Isaac Berzin and his colleagues were able to see the causes and effects of these problems, and create a potentially amazing opportunity for addressing them. This ability to observe not only helps create opportunities but also helps ensure that the correct causes of the problem are addressed. If you quickly react to a situation and skip this step, you may end up solving the wrong problem.

For example, in 1986 there was a large fish kill in Bayou Black, Louisiana. When the authorities were notified of the problem they could have easily run with their first assumption that toxins leaked into the water killing the many fish. By doing this though, they would have failed to address the real cause of the

problem. Instead, they took time to carefully observe the situation, and eventually discovered that the fish fatalities weren't the result of toxins, but rather a lack of dissolved oxygen in the water. Dense vegetation had covered much of the water's surface, keeping the sunlight from penetrating. And as a result, the underwater algae were unable to produce the much needed oxygen that the fish depended on. Treating the water for toxins before fully observing the situation would have led to an ineffective solution.

If carefully observing a problem before acting on it seems like common sense to you, why do you think people often skip this important step? Can you list a few reasons?

Perhaps you listed cell phones or technology which can distract us in many instances. Or maybe a sense of urgency hurries our thinking process. Or you might have listed political or religious beliefs that can limit our ability to fully observe a situation. What distracts you from fully observing in your day to day life?

One of the traits of skilled critical and creative thinkers is the ability to deal with distractions so that they can fully observe the problems they face. What do you need to do to harness the distractions that interfere with you observing the problems you face in your life?

Let's look at a group of talented teens who focused their observation skills to creatively comment on both the environment and social climate they face in the 21st century.

MOVERS & SHAKERS

Theatre Students, *Denver School of the Arts*

High school students from the Denver School of the Arts in Denver, Colorado wrote and staged a production, "The Inconvenient Truths," playing off of Al Gore's title from his film on global climate change. The students explored their observations of both the personal and planetary challenges they face today. Together they wrote and integrated fourteen scenes covering topics ranging from terrorism, to a

Photography credit: Diane Lather Belfour

culture steeped in body-image, to commentary on the separation of church and state, to global climate catastrophes.

The cast raised enough money to take their production on tour. They performed at the world's largest theatre festival in Edinburgh, Scotland, where they received glowing reviews. One critic who writes for *The Scotsman* said, "The content is terrific, the staging excellent, and the quality of performance truly moving; and if these magnificent, funny, angry, humble, self-aware kids speak of the whole of their generation, then there's some hope for the future, after all."

These students observed their world, put their ideas into action, and garnered international attention, demonstrating leadership and hope for the future. We hope that you too will commit to making your own observations so that you can positively affect the world around you.

POWERFUL QUESTIONS FOR DISCUSSION

1. What observations can you make about how the natural environment affects you? (allergies, humidity and your skin, SAD—seasonal affective disorder, etc.)
2. What do you observe about the political process in our country and how it affects our leaders' abilities to deal with environmental issues?
3. Think about some recent natural disasters (Hurricane Katrina, the 2008 earthquake in the southwest region of China, the 2004 tsunami in Southeast Asia). What observations could have been made before the disasters occurred that could have prompted action to lessen their negative impact?
4. Why do you think observation skills are important for students to master as 21st century learners?

BUILDING SKILLS
FOR THE TWENTY-FIRST CENTURY

Challenging Your Thinking

OBSERVING YOUR LIFE

Take this opportunity to slow down and use your critical eye to observe various areas in your life. Use the following questions to help prompt powerful observations:

- What do your senses tell you?
- What has changed over time?
- How do you feel?
- Do others observe this situation in the same way you do?
- What is positive/negative about this observation?

Family

Your most difficult class

Your closest friend

Expectations for yourself

Your environment

Your health

Others' expectations of you

Your personality

Your greatest strength

Your favorite teacher

Practicing What You Learned

MAKING OBSERVATIONS

We've discussed how scientists have observed our changing environment and how our use of energy might be affecting these changes. This activity involves observing how you use energy in your day to day life.

The term carbon footprint is often used to measure the impact of human activity on the environment. The carbon footprint measures the amount of greenhouse gasses that are produced by various human activities (riding on planes, heating houses, etc) or by the consumption of products that require energy for their production and shipment.

Several websites exist that can help you calculate your estimated carbon footprint. Before visiting these websites, observe some of your and your family's energy consumption habits. You will need to discuss some of these questions with your parents to determine the following answers:

- How many people live in your household?
- What much do you generally pay per month for electricity, natural gas, and propane?
- What type of car do you (or your parents) drive?
- What are the car's make, model and year?
- How many miles a year on average do you drive?
- If you fly, how many trips do you take a year?

If you have access to a computer, you can find various websites that will calculate your carbon footprint with the above information.

Try: www.climatefriendly.com
www.Carbonfund.org
www.conservation.org/Carboncalculator

Next, observe how people are reducing their carbon footprint. You can research this by looking on the internet, reading articles in your paper, calling your congressman or congresswoman's office, interviewing people you know, etc. Make a list of the ways that most impress you.

Finally, write an action plan for how you can apply these observations to reduce your carbon footprint:

- in the next week
- in the next month
- in the next year.

Putting Your Heads Together

FACING THE WORLD'S GREATEST PROBLEMS

Global warming & carbon dioxide emissions. Divide into teams of four. Imagine you and your teammates have been appointed by the President of the United States to review policy on carbon dioxide emissions.

As a team:

- Identify the problem.
  - Why is it a problem? What are the costs of not addressing the issue?
- Make observations.
  - What is resulting from the problem? What are the detrimental effects? Are the effects escalating?
- Analyze the problem.
  - What are the causes producing the effects you're observing? What connections can you make about this problem to other problems?
  - What are other countries doing to address the issue? How do carbon dioxide emissions differ from other environmental problems?
- Seek solutions to address the causes of the problem.
- Generate ideas to treat the negative effects that already exist from the problem.
- Write a formal report to the President summarizing your findings and recommendations. Present your report to the class.

Get Out of the Dogma House

43 Nothing clouds your decision-making abilities like dogma. Example: none other than Plato himself dictated that the circle was the perfect form for celestial movement, and for the next two thousand years, astronomers said that planetary orbits were circular—even though their observational data suggested otherwise. Even Copernicus used circles in his heliocentric model of the universe. Only after much soul-searching did Kepler use the ellipse to describe the heavenly paths. **Everyone has externally imposed "shoulds" and values that influence their thinking. What dogma is clouding your mind?**

3

Creative Whack Pack cards reprinted courtesy of Roger van Oech, © 2007. Visit creativethink.com.

how to question

Once you take time to identify and observe a problem, the next step for optimizing your critical and creative thinking is to generate questions. These are different from the basic "why" questions you ask when you first come upon a problem. These are deeper, probing questions that help you assess the problem, make connections with what you already know, recognize potential patterns, and brainstorm solutions.

In essence, questions are the bridge which moves you from the problem into the solution.

Stephen King, the famous author of blockbusters including *Carrie*, *The Green Mile* and *The Children of the Corn* series, takes a walk everyday as part of his creative thinking process. These walks provide the opportunity for him to ask questions which shake up his thinking and allow his mind to wander as he creates his stories. They keep him from getting stuck. Similarly, asking questions is a way to keep your mind from getting stuck. Think of it as taking your mind for a walk, an opportunity to get your mind in motion.

The great mathematician and scientist, Sir Isaac Newton, wrote about the three laws of motion. His first law, the Law of Inertia, states that every object persists in its state of rest, or uniform motion in a straight line, unless it is compelled to change that state by forces impressed on it. In other words, an object that is stationary or moving in one set direction will remain this

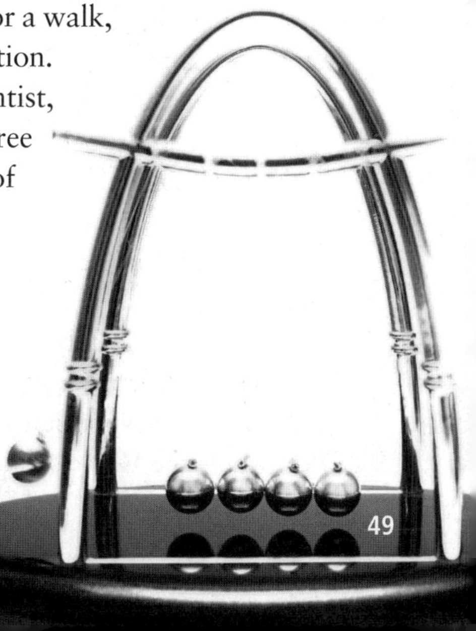

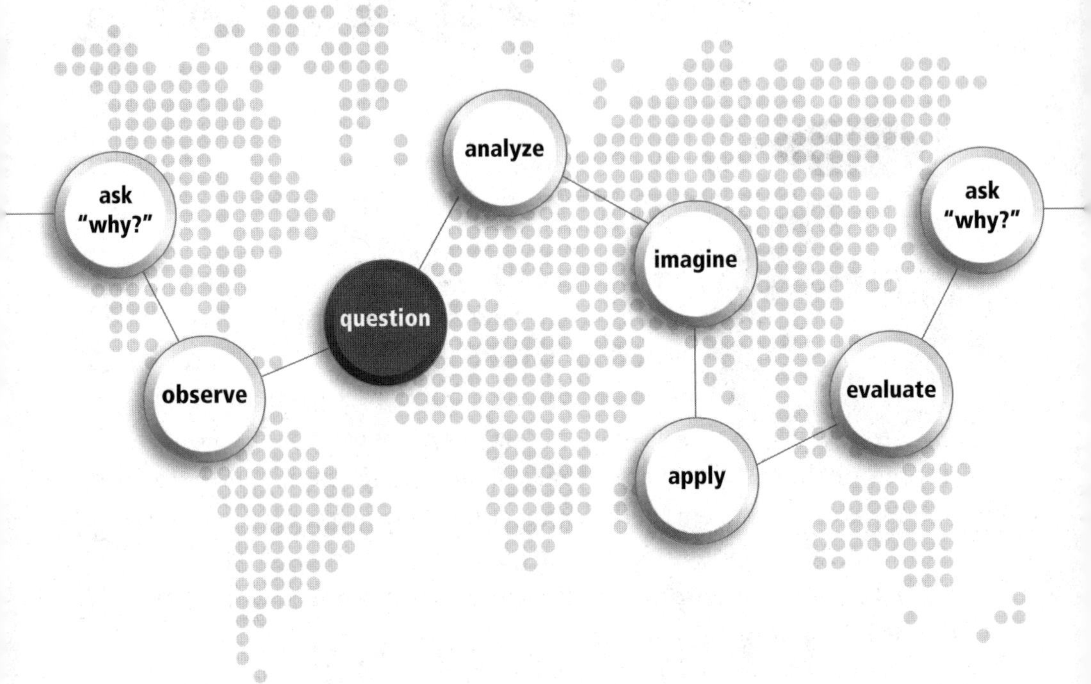

way forever unless something comes along and pushes or pulls on it.

So how does this relate to critical and creative thinking and problem solving? Picture how you think when you deal with a problem. Your mind can remain static, stuck in old solutions and patterns of thought. Perhaps you generate the same solution over and over and over. Questions then become the force impressed upon your thinking, the factor that changes or dislodges your thoughts and propels them in new directions. Questions become the "push and pull" in your thinking, helping you wrestle with new ideas and creative solutions to problems.

Because asking questions generates movement in your thinking process, we will explore this chapter through the lens of motion. Let's begin by looking at the questions Mr. George Washington Gale Ferris, Jr. asked in 1893 as he created an attraction for the World's Columbian Exposition in Chicago, more commonly known as the World's Fair.

GREAT THINKERS FROM HISTORY

George Ferris, Jr.

Mr. Ferris, Jr. was an engineer and bridge builder from Pittsburgh, Pennsylvania. He later started his own company to test and inspect metals used for railroads and bridges. While at a meeting to plan the upcoming World's Fair to be staged in Chicago, he was presented with a challenge to build something spectacular that guests of the fair would never forget.

Only years before in 1889, Paris hosted a world's fair and unveiled the Eiffel Tower, a huge engineering feat that stood 1,047 feet high, the tallest building in the world at the time. So the Americans wanted to rival the Eiffel Tower by creating something even more magnificent and inspiring. And they called Mr. Ferris, Jr. to the task.

What questions do you think Mr. Ferris, Jr. might have asked?

____

____

____

Mr. Ferris questioned whether simply building a taller structure would give America the prestige it was looking for. But what if he could create a moving tower? This question suddenly unleashed his creativity, and from here he continued:

- What did he know about other fair attractions?

This question helped him connect what he was trying to understand with what he already knew. He knew that the Merry-Go-Round was always popular, generating large revenues. It was a relatively simple structure, and it moved. So he continued asking himself the following questions.

- How could he take a horizontal wheel and turn it in a vertical plane?
- How could he build towers to support such a wheel?
- How could seats be attached to the wheel carrying people up into the air so that they could observe the entire fair?
- What would propel the giant wheel in circles?
- How would the wheel be held still to load and unload passengers?
- How would the wind affect the structure's stability?
- How could the structure be tested without injuring people?

The first Ferris wheel, Chicago 1893

Rumor has it that Mr. Ferris, Jr. drew a sketch of his idea on a cocktail napkin that very same night at dinner. And within five months 2,100 tons of materials were transported, forged and hoisted into place. Carts were hung from the wheel's arms, where 2,160 people could ride at a time. Two steam engines were put in place to power the wheel that was designed to lift people 264 feet high so that they could witness the entire fair in action.

When the Ferris wheel opened to the public on June 21, 1893, Mr. Ferris, Jr. gave a speech noting that "he'd gotten the wheels out of his head and made them a living reality;" in other words, he put his ideas into motion, all by asking the right questions.

And it is said that the first Ferris wheel was built without one change to this original design that he drew on the cocktail napkin.

Ferris wheels can now be found in most major cities across the world. The Singapore Flyer, which is currently the largest in operation, opened in 2008 and reaches 541 feet, or 42 stories, high!

ASSESSING YOUR QUESTIONING SKILLS

George Ferris used questions to launch his ideas into motion. How well can you question your ideas to build a bridge from problem to solution? You can test your skills on the following assessment where you'll be asked to use your imagination to answer a prompt. Then generate five additional questions for each of your answers that you can use to explore your response.

If you could invent a new amusement park ride that moves, what would it be?

____

Now list five questions you can ask about your response.

a. ______________________________
b. ______________________________
c. ______________________________
d. ______________________________
e. ______________________________

If you could create a unique vehicle for transportation, what would it be?

____

Now list five questions you can ask about your response.

a. ______________________________
b. ______________________________
c. ______________________________
d. ______________________________
e. ______________________________

If you could invent a personal flying machine, what would it be like?

____

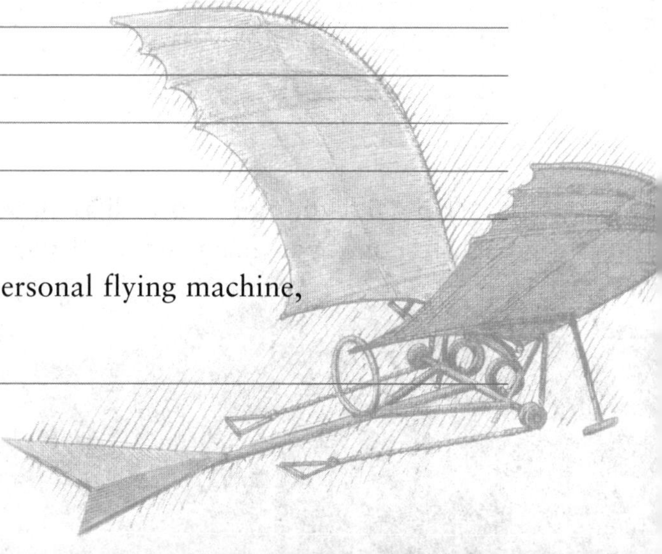

Now list five questions you can ask about your response.

a. __________

b. __________

c. __________

d. __________

e. __________

If you could create another appendage on your body to help you move, what would it be like?

____

Now list five questions you can ask about your response.

a. __________

b. __________

c. __________

d. __________

e. __________

If you could create a time travel machine, what would it be like?

____

Now list five questions you can ask about your response.

a. __________

b. __________

c. __________

d. __________

e. __________

How did you do? Was it difficult to generate questions for each response you imagined? Did your questions lead you to new insights or offer you new perspectives?

Now go back and review each of your questions. How many can be answered with a "yes" or "no"? Do you find the questions that can not be answered with a "yes" or "no" force you to think more deeply? Because deeper thinking is our goal for this book, let's take time to discuss how powerful questions initiate such thinking.

asking powerful questions

One of the first lessons every aspiring journalist learns before conducting interviews is never to ask "yes" or "no" questions. The reason is that these questions rarely serve as an inroad for further reflection or discussion. They abruptly stop the thinking or conversation.

A more powerful question is one that is open-ended; that doesn't require a specific answer. Consider the difference between asking, "Do you think this is a good idea?" and "What are your thoughts on this idea?" The first question calls for a simple yes or no, while the second questions allows for a more detailed response.

Powerful questions can help engineers create new structures and aspiring journalists report breaking news. But they also help teenagers like you move through challenging times to make the best decisions possible. Asking questions is a life skill that will bolster your critical and creative thinking and can be applied to every area of your life. Because they are so important, it is worth taking a moment to reflect on what makes a question powerful.

A POWERFUL QUESTION INTRIGUES

A question that intrigues opens your mind. It piques your curiosity and stimulates new ways of thinking. This type of question usually can't be answered quickly, but instead requires you to look at various meanings and implications.

Consider the intriguing question "What will it take for you to be a success in your own eyes?" To answer this you'd have to first define what success means to you, as opposed to others. Then you'd have to reflect on what it will take for you to achieve success. The question lends itself to deeper thinking and calls for you to take ownership of the answer, as only you can generate an authentic response to it.

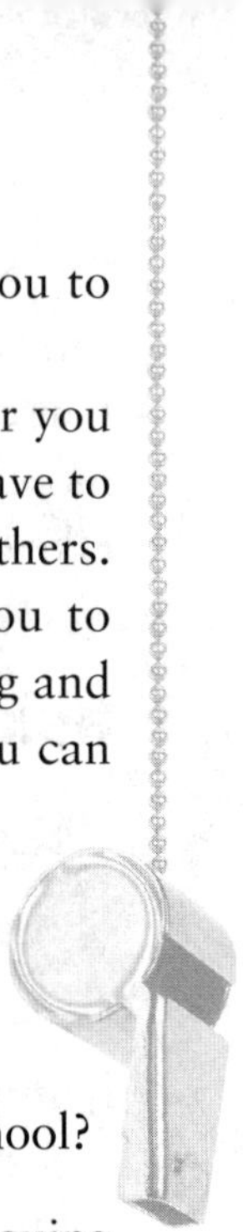

Trying it out . . .

The following question calls for a "yes" or "no" response:

_____ Do you want to move to another city after high school?

Can you transform this "yes" or "no" question into an intriguing one that calls for more complex thinking and reasoning?

____

____

____

A POWERFUL QUESTION DIRECTS

A question that directs will channel your thinking along a path. Have you ever been asked to write a response to a question that is vague and unclear? It's difficult to formulate a focused essay when the prompt fails to give you direction.

Consider if you were asked either "Do you like your friends?" or "What are the qualities your friends have that inspire you?" Which question requires you to think more deeply? The first question is fairly simple and could be asked as conversation filler. But if you are directed to reflect on your friends' inspiring qualities, you're being called to think specifically about

what you value in friendship, whether or not your friends possess these values, and why these values matter to you.

Trying it out . . .

List a powerful question you have recently asked, or been asked, that clearly directed a well thought out response. If you can't come up with one, make one up. For example, your friend wants to quit the soccer team. Instead of asking, "Do you really want to leave the team?" you could offer a more powerful question such as "What are the pay offs of no longer playing soccer?"

A POWERFUL QUESTION MOTIVATES

A powerful question motivates you, calling you to action. Such questions require you to draw answers from deep within yourself. They inspire you by focusing on what is possible through change. If your responses truly come from your inner thoughts and values, you'll be much more likely to commit to your solutions because they belong to you.

Trying it out . . .

Think about an area in your life where you feel stuck and need motivation. Now list three powerful questions about where you are and where you'd ultimately like to be. Respond to each of your questions. Finally, circle the question that would best motivate you to take action.

For example, imagine you want to move into an advance placement math class next year but you've resisted taking the necessary steps to enroll. You are supposed to register for your new schedule next week. You might ask yourself:

- What opportunities will open up for me by moving into an advanced placement class?
- How will this change bolster my self-esteem and worth?
- How can I reward myself for taking on this extra challenge?
- Why do I keep resisting the steps I must take to make this move?
- What will failing to make this schedule change cost me in the long run?

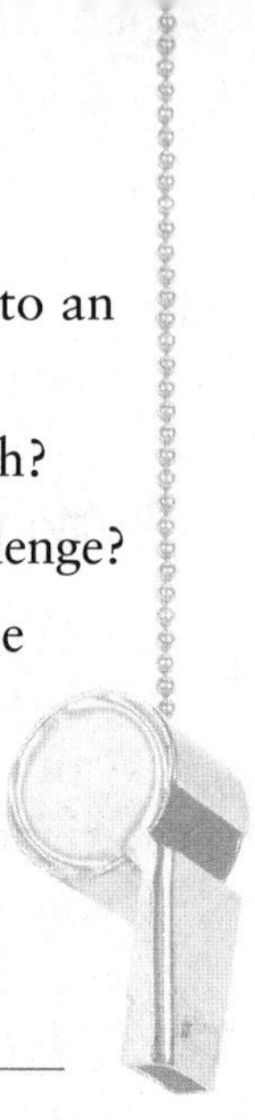

Area of feeling stuck and needing motivation

____

Motivating questions and responses:

1. ____

   ____

2. ____

   ____

3. ____

   ____

A POWERFUL QUESTION REVEALS

A powerful question exposes ideas, thoughts and perspectives that may have never been considered. These questions cut through layers and get to the heart of a matter by demanding deeper reflection and self-examination.

For example, imagine someone asking you, "Do you want to make a lot of money?" You could quickly answer yes or no without revealing much about your attitudes, your dreams, your values, or your goals.

Trying it out . . .

Instead of answering "Do you want to make a lot of money?" respond to this question:

"What will financial success give you as an adult?"

Now consider what your response reveals about you. If you claimed that financial success will give you the opportunity to travel and see the world, your sense of adventure has been revealed. If you responded that money will allow you to care for a family, it reveals your sense of responsibility. Answering that financial success will give you peace of mind so that you never have to worry, a desire for security is revealed. As you can see, a powerful question reveals so much more than a simple "yes" or "no" question does.

A POWERFUL QUESTION RESONATES

Often, a powerful question will suspend your racing mind. They create a moment to pause and reflect. Perhaps you'll experience an "ah-ha" moment, or a light bulb will click on in your head, shedding new light on your situation.

These questions often strike a chord inside you. They are the questions that linger; the ones you can ask yourself time and again; the questions which never outlive their usefulness.

Consider the question, "What are you willing to give up so that you can succeed at your goal?" This type of question can suspend your thinking, shift your perspective on your process, and be applied to many areas of your life whether you are considering schoolwork, relationships, or a desire to compete on a sports team.

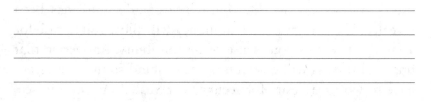

Trying it out . . .

Imagine that one of your close friends has become heavily involved with drugs. After several encounters with the law and an episode that landed her in the hospital, she comes to talk to you about her problem.

What are some powerful questions that might resonate with your friend?

If you simply ask her, "Do you like getting high?" she might respond yes, maybe, sometimes, etc., and then elaborate from there. But consider asking her questions such as:

- "What is getting high costing you?"
- "In ten years, what do you want your life to look like?"
- "What are you doing now to help you achieve these goals?"
- "How are drugs interfering with your goals?"

These questions will more likely strike a chord. They'll stimulate her thinking, requiring her to weigh the costs and benefits of her behavior and consider how the choices she's making are affecting her in the short and long term.

By learning to ask powerful questions that resonate, motivate, direct and reveal, you'll discover important information that will help you address the problem at hand—a crucial step in the critical and creative thinking process. And mastering the ability to ask questions in your personal life will ultimately help you as you successfully transition into the working world.

Let's look at how the scientist Dr. Gunther von Hagens used powerful questions in his work to study human anatomy in motion.

INNOVATIONS
CHANGING THE WORLD

Dr. Gunther von Hagens (1945-) revolutionized methods for dissecting and studying the human body after a person is deceased. When he began this work, human bodies were being dissected for scientific research, and they were often preserved by being cut and hung in sections in transparent blocks of plastic. These plastic blocks lengthened the time the bodies could be studied before they began decomposing. However this method did not allow scientists the opportunity to touch and handle the bodies. It also failed to reveal how bodies appear while in motion, which became his ultimate goal.

After acknowledging the problem and observing the current methods for body preservation and dissection available to him, Dr. von Hagens began asking questions to develop better techniques for studying human anatomy with cadavers.

If you were presented with this task what questions might you ask?

Some of the questions Dr. von Hagens considered were:

- How can I slow down the body's decomposition after death?
- How can I dissect and preserve the bodies so that I can handle and manipulate them?
- How can I use cadavers to explore human anatomy in motion?
- How can I make use of the plastic that slows down the body's decomposition?

The Skateboarder, 2005

Copyright: Gunther von Hagens, Institute for Plastination, Heidelberg, Germany, www.bodyworlds.com

Dr. von Hagens began to experiment with a procedure later named plastination. By asking himself how plastic blocks preserved the bodies, he came up with an idea to inject plastic directly into the cells of a cadaver. This procedure immediately stopped the decomposition, making the cells rigid and causing them to hold their permanent form. This process also allowed him to directly handle the bodies.

Over the past few decades, Dr. von Hagens has fine-tuned the plastination process, and more than 400 institutions in 40 countries have adopted the method for medical instruction. He advocates his preservation techniques all over the world and continues to champion its practicality in the face of religious and philosophical opposition.

He created the famous BODY WORLDS exhibit which has traveled across the globe, showcasing bodies treated with his techniques. These figures illustrate human anatomy in motion including: dancing, ski jumping, ice-skating and skateboarding. Although plastination is a controversial procedure and relies on people willingly donating their bodies for dissection and public exhibition upon death, it has revolutionized the way we view and understand the human body.

asking questions saves time and energy

The questions Dr. von Hagens asked led him from old ways of dissection to revolutionary methods for understanding the body in motion. However, powerful questions can simply be used to save you time and energy. If you are given a problem, stopping to ask questions might feel like precious time is slipping through your hands. But consider this story.

Carl Freidrich Gauss (1777-1855), is known as one of the three greatest mathematicians of all times. When he was young he had an elementary school teacher who instructed the students to add all the numbers from 1 to 100 together to find their sum. Thinking it would take some time for the students to calculate the answer, the teacher tried to step out of the classroom for a break. But Gauss immediately shot up his hand claiming he had the answer. Impossible, the teacher thought. But sure enough Gauss had completed the calculation in only a few seconds. Do you know how?

Before reading on, take a moment to try the problem yourself.

1 + 2 + 3 + 4 + ... 96 + 97 + 98 + 99 + 100 = ???

When Gauss received this problem he paused to ask himself a few questions instead of immediately adding up the numbers.

- What did he know about these numbers?
- What patterns were present?
- How could he move the numbers around to make an easier problem?

He saw that adding 1 and 100 together gave him 101. Again, he added 2 and 99 together and got 101, and 3 and 98 gave him 101. By stopping to ask himself these questions he observed an emerging pattern—that the first and last number added up to 101, the second and second to last number added up to 101, and so on. Immediately he understood that because he had 100 numbers total, this pattern would result in 50 sums of 101. So he multiplied 50 X 101 and arrived at the correct sum of 5050, saving himself much time and headache, much to the surprise of his instructor!

Where else can we ask questions to help us move through life with greater ease?

THINKING ON THE CUTTING EDGE

Have you ever watched birds in motion, flying in a "V" formation? For thousands of years, pelicans, gulls and geese have flown in this formation, taking advantage of aerodynamic benefits that result from flying slightly behind and to the side of the bird immediately ahead of them. In these positions they get caught in an "up-washed induced flow" that allows them to use less energy. During their migration flights, the birds regularly switch positions in the formation, all taking turns in the lead position which demands more energy. As a result, this formation allows the birds to fly further and more efficiently than if they were to travel alone.

Knowing this about birds' flying formations, what questions can you ask that might save humans time and energy?

____

____

____

Scientists and engineers from the NASA Dryden Flight Research Center have asked the following questions to help them apply the birds' efficient flying relationship to aircraft:

- How can we use technology to create the same "up-washed induced flow" for airplanes traveling alone?
- How can these flying efficiencies save on fuel costs and lengths of flights?
- How can these flying efficiencies be used to benefit commercial aircraft, military aircraft, procedures for refueling in the air, and the formation flying of satellites?

The science behind this thinking is quite complicated, but in short, these engineers calculated the aerodynamic benefits from bird formations and experimented with these results by applying them to real planes flying in formations. Now they are working to create an autopilot program that can simulate these aerodynamic benefits for planes flying solo. Some of the current studies have shown that such technology could save a commercial airliner flying roundtrip daily from Los Angeles to New York a reduction of more than $500,000 in fuel costs each year, as well as reducing carbon dioxide emissions by 10% each year.

Sources: http://findarticles.com, www.nasa.gov/centers/dryden/pdf/874k/main_h-2502.pdf

questions for everyday life

As you've seen, asking questions can lead to great "ah-ha!" moments, or simply offer new perspectives on problems. But regardless, they create motion, moving the brain from problem to solution mode. Questions shift you from reacting to a problem to creating a solution. Think of it this way:

Questions move the "c" from reacting to creating.

What exactly does this mean? Often, when we face a problem, we quickly react to it. By pausing to observe and then ask relevant questions, we engage our critical and creative thinking skills to generate the best solution possible, so that we are not reacting in response, but instead, **creating** a solution—a very different way of moving through life.

Imagine you auditioned to play the drums in your school band and discovered that you were not accepted. You could react to defeat by marching out of school and swearing you'll never audition again. Or, you could examine the situation and ask yourself: How prepared was I for the audition? Did I follow all the instructions? Was I dressed appropriately? What was my competition? What will be my chances if I continue to practice another year and try again? What skills do I need to improve? Etc. By going through this process, you might decide not to quit playing and create a different response to your defeat.

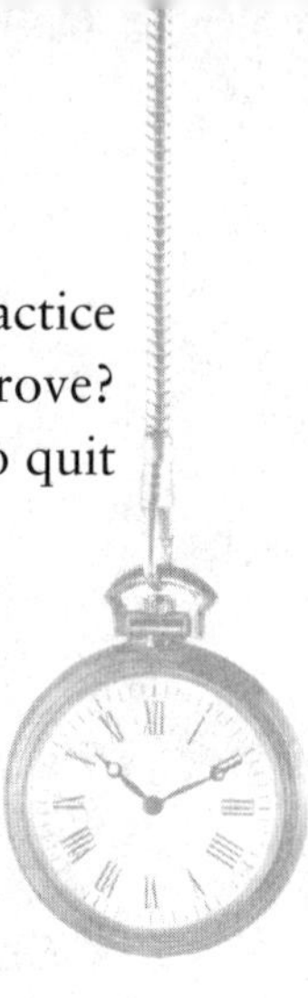

TAKE A MOMENT TO REFLECT

Describe a time when you reacted to a problem before taking the time to ask the right questions and respond more thoughtfully to the situation.

If you were able to relive this situation, how might you respond differently now?

Here is one example of a woman asking herself tough questions in a difficult situation, and as a result, influencing the world. Her questions simply spurred movement; movement that's mobilized millions of dollars for a cause.

MOVERS&SHAKERS

Susan Komen was dying from breast cancer. Her sister, Nancy Brinker, promised that she would find a way to speed up the research being done on the disease. However, Susan Komen passed away only a few short years after being diagnosed. During these difficult years, Nancy Brinker asked herself the following questions:

- Why isn't a cure available for my sister's disease?
- Why are so many women dying from breast cancer?
- How can I make an impact and do something in my sister's honor?

Nancy Brinker wasn't a doctor. She didn't possess the knowledge or tools to cure cancer. But she could walk. She could generate motion and mobilize others to move with her. And by walking together, they could raise money for research to one day find a cure for breast cancer.

These were the ideas that came from Nancy Brinker's questions, leading to the creation of the Susan G. Komen Race for the Cure, a grand scale event that takes place across the country. After twenty-five years, Race for the Cure has raised over $1 billion dollars for breast cancer research, education and health services. It is a prime example of one woman asking the questions to move her out of the problem and into the solution, one step at a time, so that future generations might be spared the devastation of breast cancer.

staying curious

We've discussed in detail how asking powerful questions can move you from problem to solution mode, expand your knowledge, and save you time and energy. But perhaps the most important thing you can do in this chapter is to commit to staying curious. If you remain curious about the world around you, you'll naturally develop great question asking skills.

Staying curious is a powerful social tool. For those who are shy and dread meeting new people, commit to being curious.

Ask new acquaintances questions. Genuinely seek out who they are and what they are about. There is no better way to initiate conversations, and it will prove to be one of your most powerful tools in your critical and creative thinking tool box.

The celebrated dancer and choreographer, Twyla Tharp, is always in motion. She makes her living by creating movement for dancers on stage. She calls her commitment to staying curious "scratching and sniffing." Whenever she begins creating a new dance she scratches and sniffs, digging for ideas that will help her create new productions to be performed across the world. This process has helped her create hundreds of dances and remain at the top of her profession for over forty years. It can help you, too.

So be hungry. Scratch, sniff and dig for information around you. Search diligently for answers. You are growing up in a world that is rapidly changing. By staying curious and asking yourself questions to jumpstart your critical and creative thinking, you'll be able to move through the challenges you'll face in your personal, academic and professional life.

POWERFUL QUESTIONS FOR DISCUSSION

1. In what areas of life do you move with ease? What questions can you ask about your performance in these areas that can shed light on your personal strengths?

2. When have you asked a significant question that moved you out of a problem and into a solution? What would have happened if you hadn't asked the question?

3. When there is a sweeping change of thought or attitude, we call it a "movement." For example, the civil rights movement or the equal rights movement. What do you predict to be the next major social movement for our country? What will be the thinking behind it?

4. Why is it important in this fast paced 21st century not to be limited by old ways of thinking? What questions do you think older, established companies are asking to keep up with the continuing waves of technological innovation?

BUILDING SKILLS FOR THE TWENTY-FIRST CENTURY

Challenging Your Thinking

CREATING A QUESTION MAP

For many, roller coasters are the ultimate amusement park ride. Have you ever wondered who invented the roller coaster, or how the cars stay on the tracks? Now is your chance to explore.

In the center circle you'll see the topic *Roller Coasters*. Your job is to ask four questions about roller coasters (feel free to ask anything you want: how are they held together, what is the history behind them, how many accidents occur on them each year, etc.)

Now it's time to scratch, sniff and dig deeper. From each of your questions, generate four more related questions. Begin this adventure and see where you land.

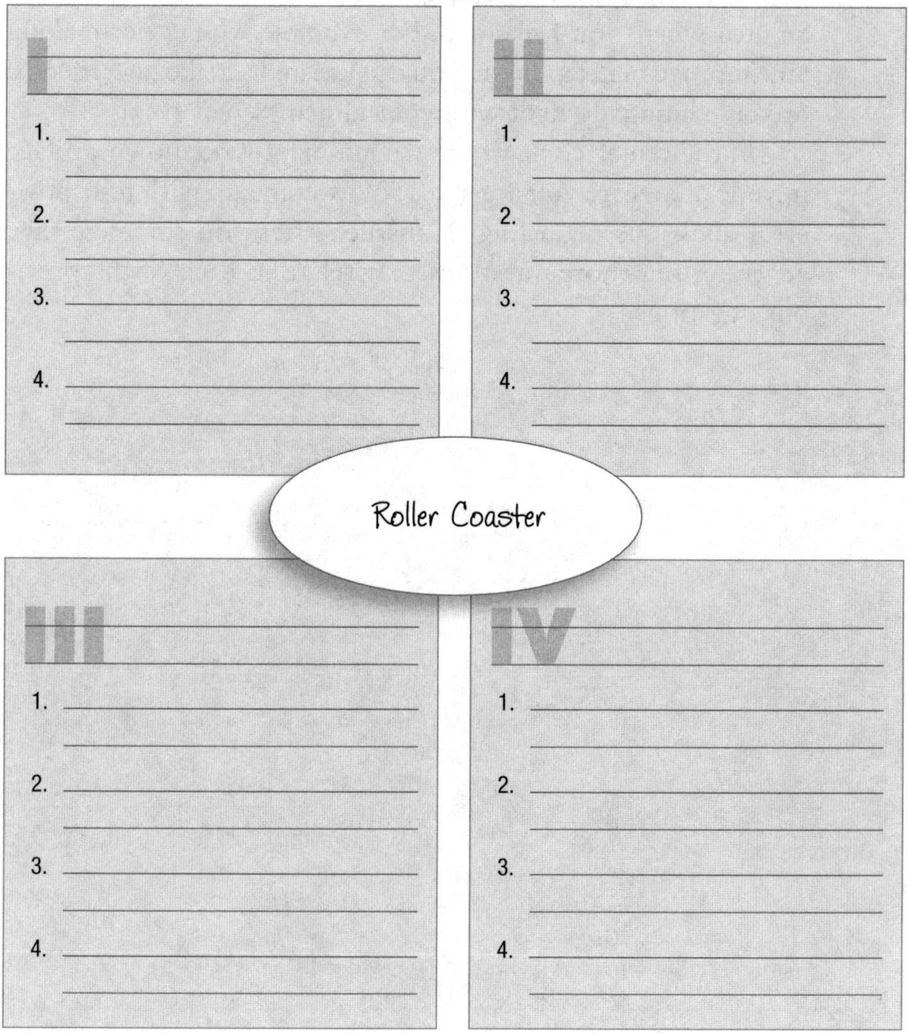

What questions did you discover that you might not have considered when you first thought about roller coasters?

Now let's apply this strategy to a personal issue. Think about an area where you feel stuck. For example, you're not making any improvements in math, you can't seem to make new friends, or you continually fight with your father.

In the center circle of the second map, write down a place in your life where you are stuck. Now come up with four powerful questions regarding this issue. After you complete this, generate four more questions that relate to each of the previous questions.

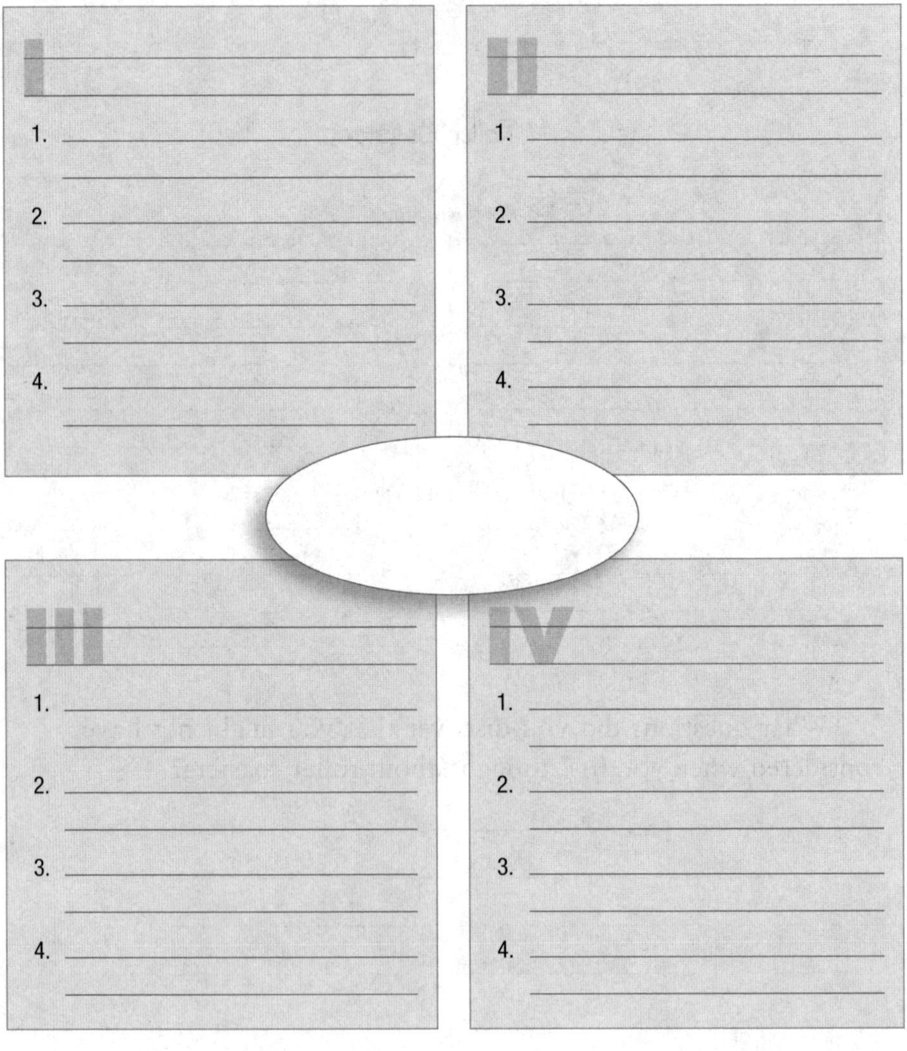

What insights did your questions give you? How have the questions opened doors to help you move out of your problem and into solution mode?

Practicing What You Learned

ASKING QUESTIONS - AN IMPROVISATION GAME

Divide into two teams. Now choose a topic (i.e. weather, football, grasshoppers, Thanksgiving, etc.).

To begin playing, the first person from team one will respond to the topic with a question. Now the first person from team two must respond to this question with a new question. This response, in question form, must relate to the previous question. Continue this process, rotating players from each team. If a player responds with a statement or answer, rather than a question, he or she must sit down. Continue until only one player remains standing. Questions may not be a simple reverse of the previous question. For example, if the question is "Why is it raining outside?" a response of "Why is it not raining?" will disqualify the player. These reversal questions are called BOOMERANGS and cause the player to be eliminated. A better response would be "Are rain clouds different than snow clouds?"

Putting Your Heads Together

SOLVING THE WORLD'S GREATEST PROBLEMS

Leaders from many countries around the world wrestle with the problem of workers moving to and from their home countries in efforts to find and retain work.

Imagine you and your classmates are appointed to a committee to examine the issues of international labor and migration rules. The questions you develop will help create greater understanding for establishing international laws that affect workers who travel across national boundaries.

Join in teams of four. Through research and dialogue with your teammates, develop a list of questions surrounding this issue.

For example

- What type of work do people travel across boundaries to do?
- How does this phenomenon affect the country where people leave?
- How does it affect the country where people arrive?
- Is this migration forced or voluntary?
- What current laws exist to promote migration?
- How are countries' taxes affected by migration?

The more questions you generate about the issue, the greater your understanding of the problem will be. Make sure to examine how movement in labor forces affects other countries around the world, not just in the U. S. Also, explore the pros and cons, not just for the workers, but for employers and citizens of both the countries receiving workers and losing workers. Once you've compiled an extensive list of questions, share them with your class. As an entire class, discuss the opinions you've started to form regarding international laws that regulate migrant workers.

Change Viewpoints

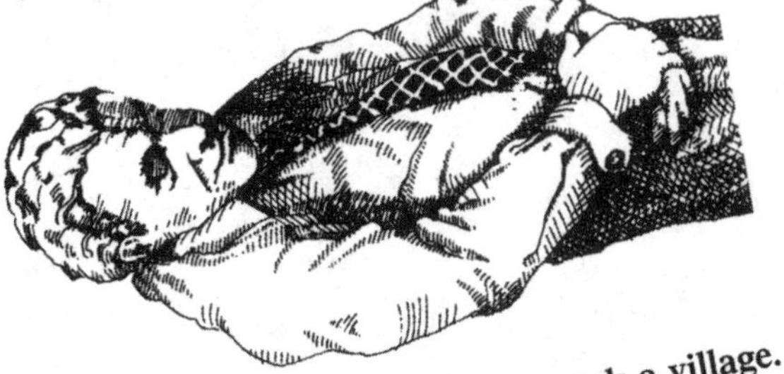

6 Long ago, a curious plague struck a village. When afflicted, its victims went into a deathlike coma, and most died within a day. The problem was that the villagers couldn't tell if a victim was dead or alive. After discovering that someone had been buried alive, an alarmed town council convened. The majority—hoping to save lives—voted to put food and water in every coffin. Another group proposed a cheaper solution: implant a stake in every coffin lid directly over the victim's heart. When closed, all doubts about the victim's condition would vanish. What differentiated the solutions were the questions used to find them. Whereas the first group asked, "What if we bury somebody *alive*," the second group asked, "How can we make sure everyone we bury is *dead*?" **Remember: the second assault on the same problem should come from a different direction. How can you change your viewpoint?**

4

Creative Whack Pack cards reprinted courtesy of Roger van Oech, © 2007. Visit creativethink.com.

how to analyze

The last two chapters addressed how to enhance your observational skills and your ability to ask powerful questions. The next step for critical and creative thinking is to take what you learned from your observations and questions, and analyze the information to develop a strategy for solving the problem at hand.

As human beings, our brains are programmed to think. Let's look at babies, who have the ability to hear, process and react to sounds, even before they're able to focus their eyes. A sudden bang can startle a newborn, just as a lullaby can calm one. An infant hears a sound, his brain interprets it—even if only in a very simplistic manner, and he then reacts.

It's not long before babies begin to listen and decipher words in terms of syllables, tone, emphasis and length. They then learn to identify words that are often repeated. And finally, they begin to interpret and label them by connecting certain words with visual images ("See the rabbit!") or people they encounter ("Mommy's here!").

By 12 months, babies generally display the ability to analyze sounds and are able to understand many words, while often producing some on their own as well. This is no minor feat! In fact, it is remarkable that when babies are born, they are predisposed to learn any one of the worlds' 7,000 languages. And it all starts with the sounds they hear at infancy. Because of this profound effect sound has on

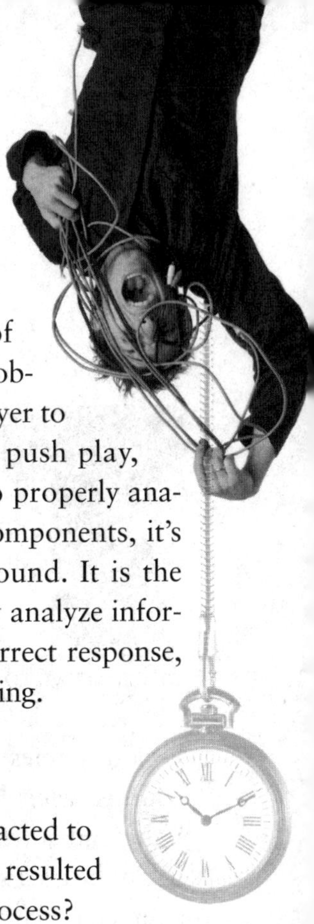

our learning, we will examine the step of analysis in the critical and creative thinking process through the lens of sound.

As we mature and our brains develop, however, we sometimes overlook this important step of analyzing information before taking action on a problem. How many of you have plugged in a DVD player to speakers and a TV, only to find that when you push play, there is no volume? If you don't take the time to properly analyze how the various cords feed into each of the components, it's easy to cross your wires and end up with no sound. It is the same with all problem solving. Failing to properly analyze information before taking action can result in an incorrect response, so this step is the cornerstone of deeper level thinking.

TAKE A MOMENT TO REFLECT . . .

Describe a time when you heard something and reacted to it without analyzing the information first. What resulted from skipping this step of the critical thinking process?

evaluating information

CHALLENGING ASSUMPTIONS AND SHIFTING PERSPECTIVES

Before we go into greater detail on how to analyze information gathered from observations and questions, let's take a moment to discuss how assumptions and perspectives can color how we interpret information.

We'll begin by discussing what an assumption actually is. An assumption is an idea we take for granted. Our assumptions generally stem from what we have learned in the past and they become beliefs that we no longer routinely question. They help us interpret

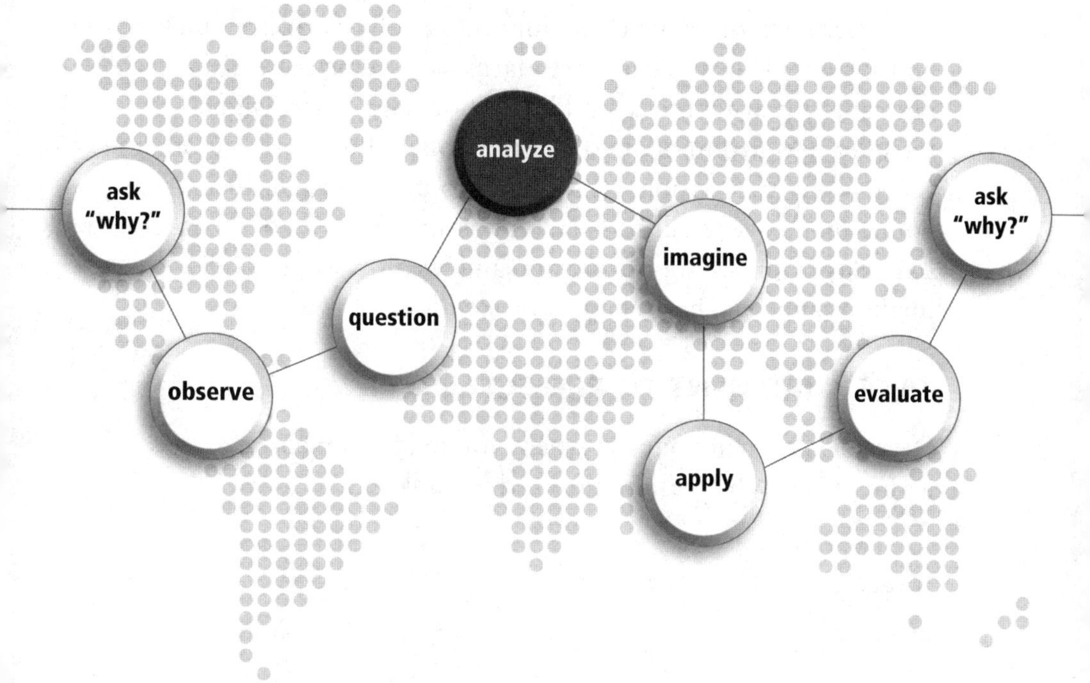

information more quickly and speed up our ability to act or react. However assumptions become problematic when they are based on misinformation or beliefs that are unjustifiable in a given situation.

For example, imagine you are sound asleep in the middle of the night and you hear your family telephone ring. You wake up, look at the clock and see it is 3:00 a.m. Your heart begins to beat faster and your mind races. Something must be wrong, you assume, knowing that no one would be calling at such an hour if this were not the case. The phone continues to ring and no one from your house gets up to answer it. You crawl out of bed, walk down the hall and lift the receiver to your ears, only to find someone from China has dialed the wrong number. In this instance, your assumption that no one would call at 3:00 a.m. unless it was an emergency, immediately affects your response (both voluntary—getting up in the dark to answer the phone, and involuntary—your heart begins racing).

There are times when assumptions help us to act quickly and safely: when we hear a fire alarm we assume there is danger and quickly evacuate a building; a burglar alarm signals an intruder and prompts us to call the police. But there are other times when assumptions can lead us to incorrect conclusions: a young man is very tall so we might assume he is a good basketball player, or seeing an elegant and wealthy supermodel, we might assume she has a happy, blessed life.

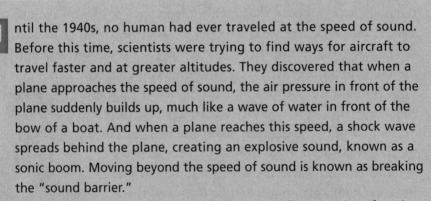

TAKE A MOMENT TO REFLECT . . .

Describe a time in your life where you made an incorrect assumption. What resulted from this thinking?

THINKING ON THE CUTTING EDGE

Until the 1940s, no human had ever traveled at the speed of sound. Before this time, scientists were trying to find ways for aircraft to travel faster and at greater altitudes. They discovered that when a plane approaches the speed of sound, the air pressure in front of the plane suddenly builds up, much like a wave of water in front of the bow of a boat. And when a plane reaches this speed, a shock wave spreads behind the plane, creating an explosive sound, known as a sonic boom. Moving beyond the speed of sound is known as breaking the "sound barrier."

In the 1930s, it was assumed that controlling an aircraft as it broke the sound barrier was impossible. A series of deadly accidents that occurred when planes attempted this feat seemed to confirm their assumptions. But a few scientists of the day challenged this line

Chuck Yeager and the X-I Aircraft

of thinking. Instead of believing that crashes were inevitable at this speed, they began experimenting with aircraft design to see how planes might be built differently to withstand this test. What they discovered was:

- planes with a smooth body shape that were slender and long were more able to handle the turbulence of the air flow conditions
- the wings of the planes needed to be shorter and thinner in relation to the plane's body to perform at these high altitudes and speeds
- the tail of the airplane needed to be controlled by the pilot to help the aircraft move through the sound barrier.

On October 14th, 1947, pilot Chuck Yeager flew the experimental X-1 aircraft at the speed of sound, reaching an altitude of 45,000 feet and becoming the first human to break the sound barrier. This example shows us how challenging assumptions can facilitate groundbreaking outcomes.

Like assumptions, it is important to understand how our perspectives affect our thinking. While an assumption is something we take as truth that affects how we end up interpreting a situation, a perspective is a lens, or mental view point, affecting how we observe a situation.

Many of you have probably seen the popular TV show *American Idol*. Each week, judges offer critical feedback to the singers regarding their performances. With four different judges,

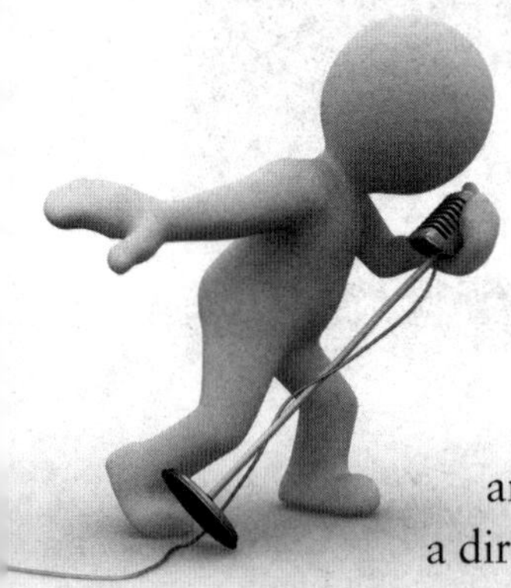

you might hear four different opinions for each song performed. This happens because each judge views the performance from their own perspective. One might evaluate it from the lens of the singer's ability to showcase their voice range and control. Another judge might evaluate it from the perspective of the performer's ability to sing across multiple genres. Or another might judge the performance on how well the singer moves on stage and engages the audience. Their final assessment is a direct result of their perspective or mental view point.

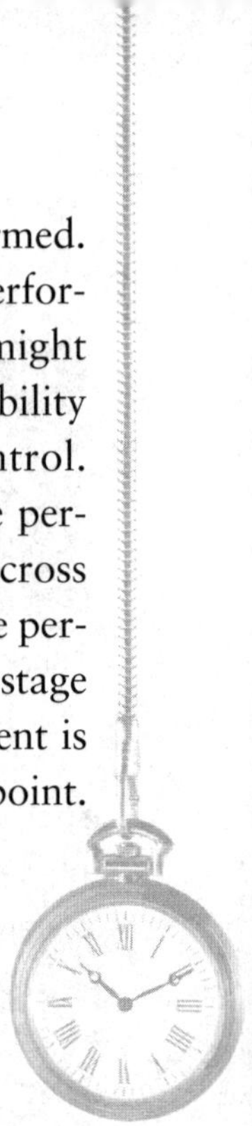

TAKE A MOMENT TO REFLECT . . .

When has your perspective clouded the way you heard something?

____

____

____

Let us take a moment to reflect on how assumptions and perspectives influence your day to day thinking.

assumptions and perspectives assessment

Remember that **assumptions** are ideas that you think to be true, which then affect how you interpret a situation.

What do you assume when someone can't speak your language?

____

What would you assume when your friend doesn't call when he or she promised?

____

When have you assumed people are laughing at you?

When have you assumed people are laughing with you?

What would you assume if you saw someone running down the street with a ski mask pulled over their face?

What do you assume when you see someone who is dirty and without shoes, walking along the street?

What do you assume when you get poor marks on a test?

What do you assume when people say they are Republican/ Democrat?

Remember that **perspectives** are mental view points through which you observe a situation.

What perspective do you take when you read the newspaper (i.e. the information is unbiased, etc)?

What perspective do you take when your parents set limitations on you?

What perspective do you take when you travel outside of your city, state or country?

What perspective do you take when you eat unfamiliar food?

What perspective do you take when you watch a movie with subtitles?

What perspective do you take when you see someone practicing a different religion from your own?

What perspective do you take when you learn about world history?

The following traditional Taoist story offers a wonderful opportunity to reflect on how our assumptions and perspectives affect our thinking about a situation.

> When an old farmer's stallion wins a prize at a county show, his neighbor calls around to congratulate him, but the old farmer says, "Who knows what is good and what is bad?" The next day some thieves come and steal his valuable animal. His neighbor comes to commiserate with him, but the farmer replies, "Who knows what is good and what is bad?" A few days later the spirited stallion escapes from the thieves and joins a herd of wild mares, leading them back to his farm. The neighbor calls to share the farmer's joy, but the farmer says, "Who knows what is good and what is bad?" The following day, while trying to tame one of the wild mares, the farmer's son is thrown and fractures his leg. The neighbor calls to share the farmer's sorrow, but the farmer's attitude remains as before. The following week, the army passes by forcibly conscripting soldiers for a war, but they do not take the farmer's son because he cannot walk. The neighbor thinks to himself, "Who knows what is good and what is bad?"

What assumptions arise in this story?

How do perspectives shift in this tale?

____

____

____

comparing, contrasting and connecting

Once you've gathered information and challenged your assumptions and perspectives, you can begin to analyze what you've discovered by comparing, contrasting and connecting the information.

LEARNING BY COMPARING

The first step is to compare the new knowledge to what you already know. To compare information, ask yourself the following questions:

- How do the facts relate to other situations?
- Where have similar behaviors and trends appeared in the past?
- What else does this situation have in common with other situations?

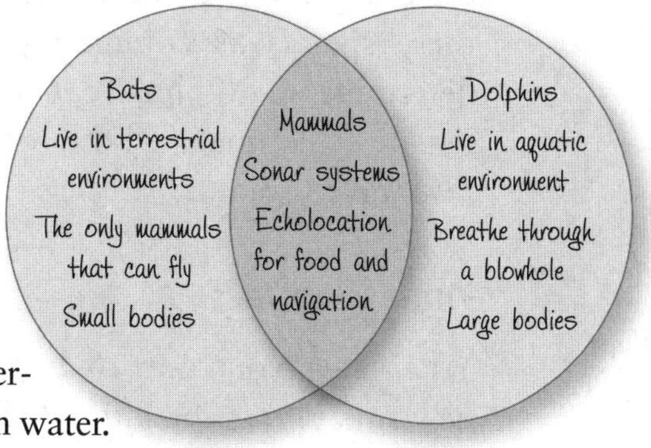

Have you ever thought about hearing underwater? The following example illustrates how great thinkers studied sound traveling through water. It goes on to discuss how scientists compared what they knew about bats to better understand how dolphins communicate in water.

Leonardo da Vinci, the famous 15th century Renaissance artist and scientist, was one of the first people to conduct sound experiments underwater by using air tubes to hear distant ships. However, it wasn't until the 1950s when scientists made great strides in understanding how sound travels underwater, and specifically, how dolphins use sounds to communicate and locate objects in their environment. Scientists did this by comparing what they were learning about dolphins to what they already knew about bats. Bats navigate their surroundings using echolocation, a method of sending out sound signals and then responding to the echoes these sounds produce.

Scientists discovered that the dolphins make rapid clicking sounds that they project in a focused beam that travels through the water. Dolphins then listen for the echo to help them know where objects are in their environment, much like bats do. These researchers also noted that mother dolphins whistle to their babies for several days after birth so that the newborns recognize the sounds as a means for communicating.

Scientists later developed the hydrophone, an underwater sound projector which delivers high-pitched sounds audible to the dolphins. They began training the mammals to respond to these signals as commands. Studies are now underway to determine if dolphins can be trained to respond to human music, by comparing how both the human ear and dolphin ear respond to sound.

Time to reflect . . .

When have you compared what you already know to a new situation and had it advance your learning?

______

______

______

LEARNING BY CONTRASTING

As with comparing, knowing how to contrast new and old information can help you deepen your understanding and learning. You can contrast information by asking yourself questions such as:

- How does this differ from what I already know?
- How are the results different from what I expected?
- What are the changes that produced different outcomes?

Be on the lookout for differences in the world around you, as they can lead to new and unexpected insights.

Pythagoras, the famous Greek philosopher from approximately 570 B.C. to 500 B.C., relied on contrasting information to make many discoveries. He is most commonly known for the Pythagorean Theorem $a^2 + b^2 = c^2$ which is named after him (although he most likely didn't prove this theorem). What many people don't know is that he was also responsible for developing what we now consider the common musical scale.

As the story goes, Pythagoras was strolling down a street when he heard a blacksmith hammering in a shop nearby. He noticed the contrasting sounds made by the hammers. Some of the hammering sounds were harmonious and other discordant. He wanted to understand why the sounds were different. So he entered the shop to examine the hammers more closely. Several of the hammers differed in size and weight. What he realized was that when hammers whose sizes were in simple mathematical relationship, meaning their masses were simple ratios or fractions of each other, they produced harmonious sounds when hammered together. However, by contrast, those hammers whose sizes did not have masses with

simple ratios or fractions, made discordant sounds when hammered at the same time.

Suddenly Pythagoras knew he was on to something: musical tones could be expressed in mathematical relationships. He then began experimenting with strings of varying lengths, contrasting the sounds when different strings were plucked together. His work and insights ultimately led to the musical scale we use today.

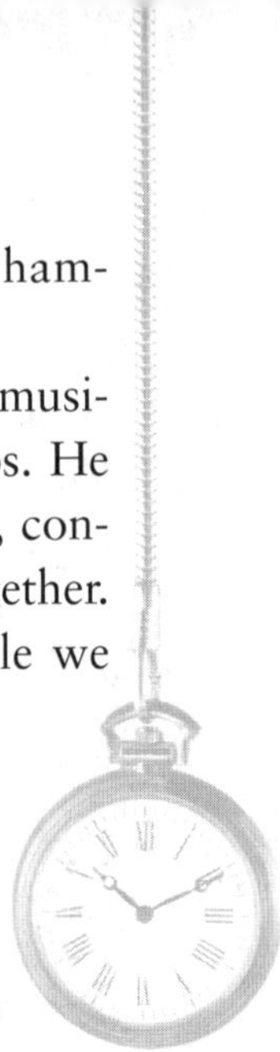

Time to reflect . . .

Describe a time when you were able to find a contrast between some new information you'd gathered and something you'd learned in your past. What was the outcome and how did this deepen your learning?

____

____

____

LEARN BY CONNECTING

One of the most significant steps to analyzing information is connecting what you already know to new information you are gathering. Connecting happens as you both compare and contrast. You're simply taking new information and finding the similarities and differences to what you already know and then building on this knowledge. By connecting new discoveries to what you've previously learned and experienced, you generate deeper thinking about a problem.

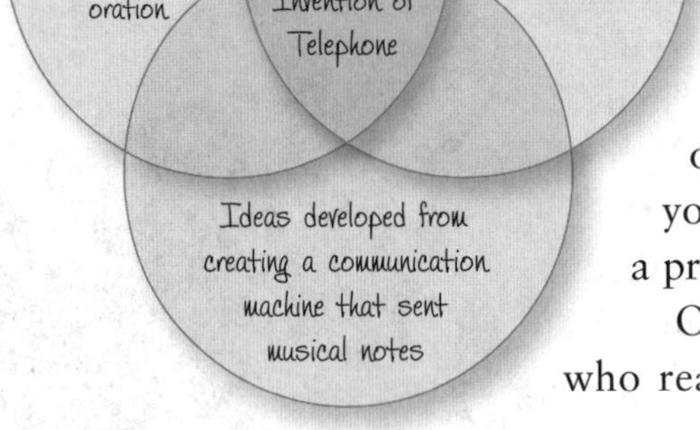

One of the most noted inventors who reached great heights by connecting information is Alexander Graham Bell. Best known for inventing the telephone, Alexander Graham Bell spent a lifetime working with the deaf and advancing means of communication for all. His mother was deaf, as well as his wife Mabel, and much of his work was inspired by connecting what he learned from living with these two women.

Communication became his focus as he taught oration and speech as a professor at Boston University. Connecting what he knew about speech and deafness, he began experimenting with devices that would allow him to communicate with both his wife and mother. He also worked on a communication machine fueled by electricity that could send musical notes a far distance.

Gathering what he'd learned from these various experiences, he set out to create a machine that could send not only musical notes, but human speech, leading him to the invention of the telephone. Had Bell set out to create the telephone without his prior experiences, he may never have ended up with such an invention. Instead, it was the result of all his early findings, connected and woven together, which ultimately led him to one of the greatest discoveries of the century.

Time to reflect . . .

When have you successfully connected new information to knowledge you previously had, and as a result deepened your learning and understanding?

Our Great Creator for this chapter successfully compared, contrasted and connected sounds as a teen to learn about music. He eventually created a unique style of guitar playing.

GREAT CREATORS OF TODAY

Trace Bundy, ACOUSTIC NINJA

Photo by Kimberly Kay Photography

Trace Bundy is an acoustic guitar player also known as the Acoustic Ninja for his fancy finger work and complex playing. This professional musician bought his first guitar at 11 years old when he and his brother each chipped in $5 to buy a used acoustic guitar. Not having the money for lessons, Trace taught himself to play by listening to others' music and creating his own songs, a perfect display of comparing, contrasting and connecting knowledge. He became interested in why different notes and chords seem to fit naturally when played together, and as a result he began exploring music theory on his own. He discovered patterns that often exist in music and gave his discoveries names such as "Traces' 7 Chord Theory," only to find out in college that his discoveries already existed and had been given complex names!

Trace pushed the boundaries of his music and discovered he could make more complex sounds using all five of his fingers, so he quit playing with a pick. He now travels around the world performing and recording his own compositions. His success is a testament to blending fine-tuned critical and creative thinking skills to his passion for music. To hear some of Trace's master guitar playing, look him up on YouTube, where he performs with Korea's child prodigy guitar player, Sungha Jung, or check out his own website at www.tracebundy.com.

In summary, this chapter has focused on the following steps for analyzing information. First, consider what assumptions you are making and what perspectives you're using to view the situation. You can ask yourself: are these assumptions and perspectives serving my learning or clouding my understanding? Next, compare and contrast the new information you've acquired to what you already know. And finally, connect this knowledge to other things you know. Once you've thoroughly analyzed your information, you can begin to strategize a solution for your problem.

But what if you take time to observe a problem, to ask relevant questions and thoroughly analyze the information you've gathered, and still can't determine a strategy for solving the problem? What do you do then? When this happens, it's time to engage your imagination. The next chapter "How to Imagine" will help you jumpstart your creative thinking skills.

BUILDING SKILLS
FOR THE TWENTY-FIRST CENTURY

Challenging Your Thinking

CREATING YOUR OWN STORY

Reread the traditional Taoist story from this chapter.

Now create your own one page story that illustrates shifts of perspective and multiple assumptions.

Practicing What You Learned

TRYING ON DIFFERENT PERSPECTIVES

Shifting perspectives. Write three sentences about the stated topic from each perspective listed. For example if the topic is education in the United States, assessments from the perspective of an orphan in Ghana might include: The classrooms have heat and there are places for all students to sit. The students have a classroom room filled with books that they can read. Hot food is served mid-day to all the students.

The sound of a baby crying:

a. a tired mother in the middle of the night
b. a family dog
c. a businessman traveling on an airplane
d. a doctor trying to diagnose the baby's illness

Hip Hop music:

a. a teenager who dances in competitions
b. a Buddhist monk

c. a senior citizen who played the violin for fifty years
d. a Reggae artist from Jamaica

Silence in the middle of the night:
a. a twelve year old home alone
b. a doctor working the overnight shift in the emergency room
c. a mother of twin infants
d. a burglar breaking into someone's home

Putting Your Heads Together

SOLVING THE WORLD'S GREATEST PROBLEMS

Maritime safety has been declared as one of the highest priorities for nations to come together to address. Countries from around the globe use the oceans to ship and receive goods, yet no one nation is responsible for establishing the laws and setting standards for seafarers and international shipping traffic. And for the U.S., the high volumes of sea traffic pose a potential threat to national security.

The U.S. Navy has developed sophisticated sonar programs for underwater navigation and the detection of enemy ships to deal with the national security concerns. However, these high powered sonar transmitters are thought to cause harm to marine life, especially dolphins and whales that use echolocation for communication, finding prey, and mating.

In November 2008 the U.S. Supreme Court ruled in favor of the Navy, allowing them to continue use of sonar in anti-submarine training sites despite its negative effects on marine life.

Working in teams of four, research this U.S. Supreme Court case and make observations about the following:

- How sonar is used in military operations
- The proven effects sonar has on sea life

Now answer the following questions to gather more information about the issue:

- What are the disadvantages of halting maritime sonar activities?
- What other means of training could be adapted in place of sonar?

What other questions can you ask to give you additional insights into the issue?

- ____________________
- ____________________
- ____________________

The next step is to analyze the information you've gathered by comparing, contrasting and connecting it to what you already know. Make sure to challenge your assumptions and perspectives as you analyze your information.

Now imagine you've been asked to share your opinions with the court. Make a presentation showing your position on these issues, giving a recommendation for solving this problem.

Try A Random Idea

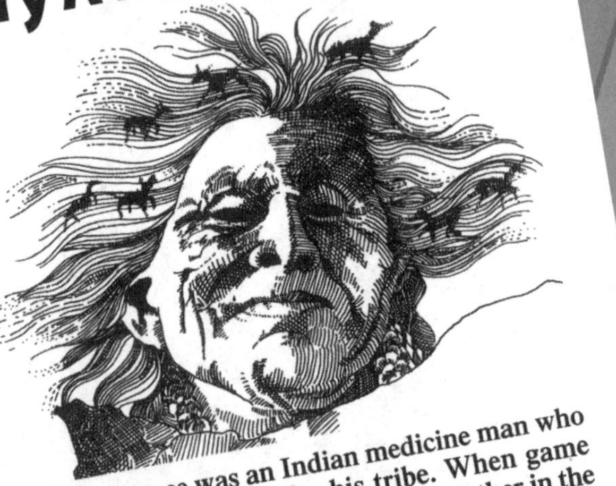

8 There once was an Indian medicine man who made hunting maps for his tribe. When game got sparse, he'd put a piece of fresh leather in the sun to dry. Then he'd say a few prayers, fold and twist it, and then smooth it out. The rawhide was now etched with lines. He marked some reference points, and a new map was created. When the hunters followed the map's newly defined trails, they usually discovered abundant game. Moral: by letting the rawhide's random folds represent trails, he pointed the hunters to places they had not looked. Stimulate your thinking in a similar way. Open any book at random and put your finger down on a word. How does it relate to what you're doing? **What random ideas can you try?**

5

Creative Whack Pack cards reprinted courtesy of Roger van Oech, © 2007. Visit creativethink.com.

how to imagine

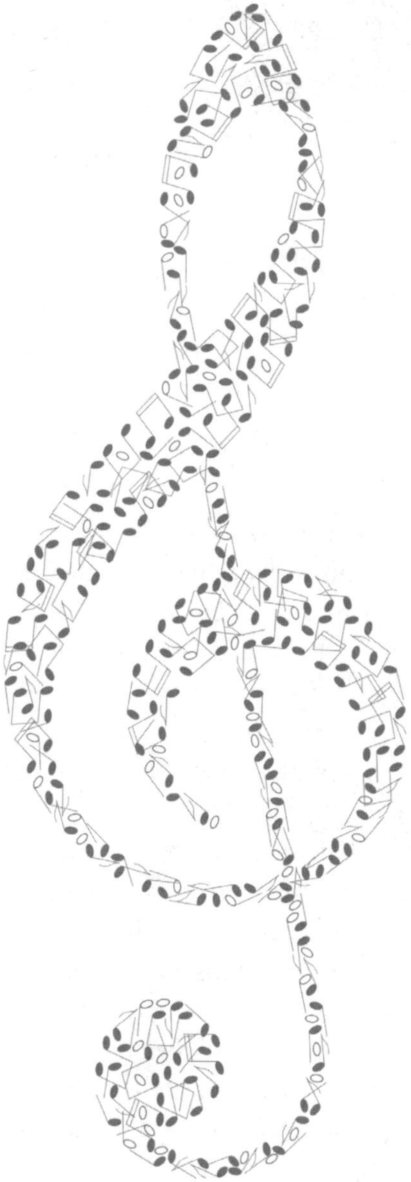

IMAGINE

Imagine there's no heaven
It's easy if you try
No hell below us
Above us only sky
Imagine all the people
Living for today . . .

Imagine there are no countries
It isn't hard to do
Nothing to kill or die for
And no religion too
Imagine all the people
Living life in peace . . .

You may say I'm a dreamer
But I'm not the only one
I hope someday you'll join us
And the world will be as one

Imagine no possessions
I wonder if you can
No need for greed or hunger
A brotherhood of man
Imagine all the people
Sharing all the world . . .

You may say I'm a dreamer
But I'm not the only one
I hope someday you'll join us
And the world will live as one

John Lennon

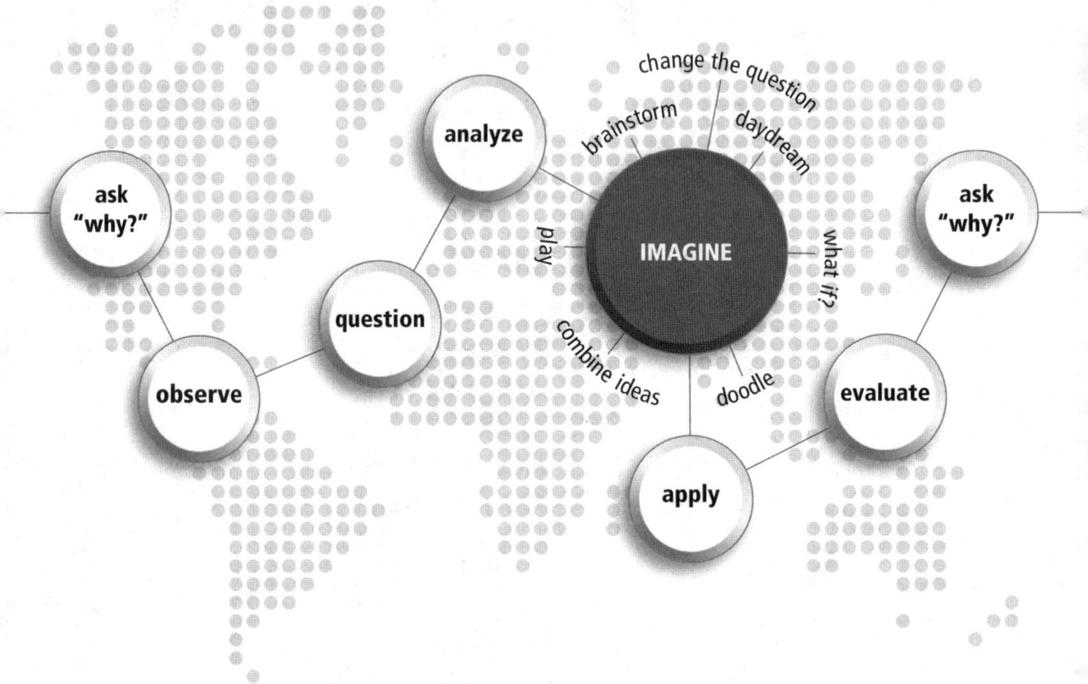

John Lennon, the famous Beatles musician who wrote these lyrics, imagined a world where peace prevails, where humans share the earth, where no one dies of hunger. This song took the world by storm, becoming one of the best-selling classics of all time.

Since this song was written, we've witnessed some extraordinary leaders rise to the challenge of creating new ways for humans to collectively work together for the good of all. Some of these great thinkers will be profiled in this chapter. But as we've moved into the 21st century, we continue to face war, hunger, terrorism and disease. And the effects of globalization have intensified many of these challenges. Perhaps now more than ever, we need to stretch our imagination and create solutions for humans to be able to successfully coexist. Because of these challenges, we are going to explore this next step in the critical and creative thinking process, *How to Imagine*, through the lens of humanity.

What if you took time to imagine? What possibilities might exist for you and others around you? You may say that you don't have a strong imagination, or that you're not the creative type. But like a muscle, your imagination grows stronger with exercise. The goal of this chapter is to offer you ways for you to cultivate your imagination.

generating ideas

Using your imagination to generate ideas is important for both critical and creative thinking. It is the step you take when you get stuck and can't solve a problem. It is the key to coming up with innovative solutions. When you imagine, you form a mental picture or visualize an idea. Once the image is imprinted in your mind, it can then be executed.

It takes time and effort to imagine. Often, a quick search for the "right" answer will inhibit your imagination that can lead to the "best" answer. To combat this, you can brainstorm to generate ideas. Brainstorming is the practice of spontaneously listing as many possible solutions to a problem as you can without censoring their feasibility. In addition to brainstorming, you can ask the following questions to jumpstart your imagination:

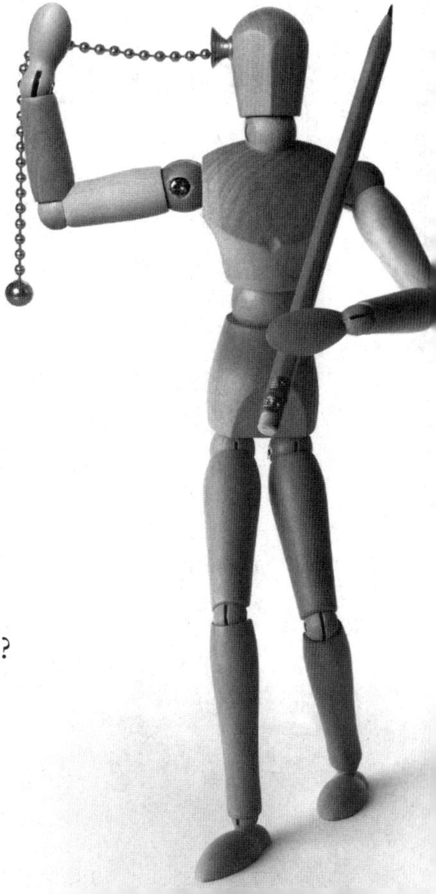

- What if?
- Why not?
- What rules can be broken?
- What parts can be eliminated?
- What can be added?
- What if we turn things upside down?

TRYING IT OUT . . .

Try creating new ideas that don't seem logical. Challenge yourself to push the boundaries of your thinking.

- Imagine a computer expressing emotion when it is happy, sad, tired, or irritated
- Imagine water flowing upstream
- Imagine plants speaking your language
- Imagine all humans are bald
- Imagine the sky turning orange at night
- Imagine children writing the laws for a city

Now ask yourself "what if?" and let your mind run wild. Create your own illogical ideas.

- *Imagine . . .* ______________________________
- *Imagine . . .* ______________________________
- *Imagine . . .* ______________________________
- *Imagine . . .* ______________________________
- *Imagine . . .* ______________________________
- *Imagine . . .* ______________________________
- *Imagine . . .* ______________________________
- *Imagine . . .* ______________________________

- *Imagine . . .* ______________________________

____

- *Imagine . . .* ______________________________

____

Now choose your favorite idea from above. What would the world look like if what you imagined became reality? Write your ideas in a short paragraph on the lines below.

____

____

____

____

____

____

Asking "what if" is a great way to get your creative juices flowing. However, posing "why not" is an equally powerful tool to help you dream big. Ivan Suvanjieff, an artist, musician and relentless dreamer, asked "why not" and as a result, created PeaceJam.

THINKING ON THE CUTTING EDGE

During the summer of 1994, Ivan Suvanjieff spent time with Latino gang members who worked the streets of a Denver neighborhood riddled with gang and drug activity. Through conversations with these teens, he realized that they not only knew the Nobel Peace Prize winner, Desmond Tutu, but that they believed in his approach of using nonviolence to create change in the world. In the midst of poverty, crime and hopelessness, Suvanjieff witnessed these teens' ability to imagine a life beyond their violent streets and embrace the spirit of greatness that Desmond Tutu embodied.

It suddenly dawned on Suvanjieff. What if teens could work together with such Nobel Peace Prize Laureates to help bring peace to communities throughout the world? Many laughed at Suvanjieff's idea. But he pressed on, asking "why not?" Why wouldn't the laureates join his efforts? Why couldn't he help today's youth recapture a sense of power and meaning in the world?

Suvanjieff shared his idea with Dawn Engle, and together they presented their vision to the Dalai Lama. The Dalai Lama jumped on board along with twelve other Nobel Peace Prize Laureates including Desmond Tutu, Aung San Suu Kyi, and President Oscar Arias. The PeaceJam Foundation was born with a mission to create a new generation of young leaders committed to positive change in themselves, their communities and the world through the inspiration of the Nobel Peace Laureates.

Since PeaceJam's beginning in 1996, more that 600,000 youth have participated, over one million service projects have been implemented by teens, and over 140 events have taken place in ten different countries. The foundation's incredible success all points back to a dream conceived on a gang-ridden street, where a young man stoked his imagination by asking "Why not?"

imagination in daily life

Suvanjieff is using his imagination to improve the world, just as you can use your imagination to enhance your daily life. We've talked a lot about using critical and creative thinking to solve problems. But it can also be applied to simply improving a situation, turning an adequate or good situation into something great. Take a moment to reflect on how you can make things better. Create a list of areas in your own life that might be improved by applying your imagination. It might be as simple as how you manage your time before you leave for school in the morning, or more complex such as how you can mobilize your friends to support your favorite cause.

1. ______________________________
2. ______________________________
3. ______________________________
4. ______________________________
5. ______________________________

As you read through the following ways to activate your imagination, keep in mind the areas in your life where you can apply these concepts.

CREATE MULTIPLE IDEAS

As you look to improve a situation, use your imagination to generate as many ideas as possible. While the old saying "your first response is usually your best" might be true in some instances, it won't in all. And you'll never know if you don't have other ideas for comparison.

While you push for multiple solutions, all your choices may not be award-winning. However, ideas can be built on other ideas. You might have a thought that leads to another thought that generates a masterful idea! Take the chance and the time to travel with

your imagination. Once you have a variety of choices to select from, you can begin to put a strategy into place.

Imagine you are on a task force responsible for reducing the number of homeless people in your city. Chances are, you wouldn't come up with only one solution to address this problem. Rather, you and your team would probably take a considerable amount of time to brainstorm, creating a list of possible tactics your city could take to address the problem.

Now, reflect on one of the challenges from your own life that you just listed. Generate five different ideas in response to the challenge. Some of your thoughts may become possible solutions to choose from, and others merely stepping stones to greater ideas.

1. ______________________________
2. ______________________________
3. ______________________________
4. ______________________________
5. ______________________________

TRY ON SOMEONE ELSE'S SHOES

If you find you're stuck and having a hard time imagining new ideas, think about how someone else might solve the problem.

Let's go back to the task force example. Your team might look at how other cities deal with homeless populations, and compare and contrast these to the circumstances surrounding your problem. Or perhaps you'd go directly to the source, and gather ideas from the homeless people themselves, or from people who recently moved off the streets. Different perspectives can inspire your thinking.

Consider one of your own challenges you listed earlier. Imagine three other people solving your dilemma. Who are they and what solutions do you envision them using?

1. ______________________________
2. ______________________________
3. ______________________________

CHANGE THE QUESTION

If you are unable to generate ideas to respond to a question, try changing the question. This tip is really just another way of looking at things differently.

In our example of the task force, your team would begin by asking, "How can we reduce the number of homeless people in our city?" But by changing the original question into the following questions, you might generate new ideas for tackling the problem:

- "How can we secure employment for the homeless?"
- "What are the factors that contribute to homelessness?"
- "What type of safety nets can we put in place for people who lose their jobs, have medical emergencies, or substance abuse problems?"
- "What incentives can we provide to homeless people to move into temporary housing?"

Changing the question helps inspire your imagination to think in different ways. Now change the wording to a personal challenge you listed above to see how it stimulates your thinking!

____

____

____

COMBINE IDEAS

There is a theory that creative thoughts most often spring from the intersection of two unconnected ideas. Think of Charles Goodyear in the 1800s who accidentally dropped a concoction he was developing on top of a wood burning stove. The mistaken result was vulcanized rubber—now used throughout the modern world!

George Harrison, another songwriter from The Beatles, challenged himself to open a random book, read a line, and write a song based on the words he read. So turning the pages, his eyes first rested on "gently weeps" which he used to create The Beatles famous hit "While My Guitar Gently Weeps." Sometimes it's the limitations a second idea places upon the first that stirs the creative juices.

Continuing with our homeless example, your task force might combine an idea for an early intervention education program for people who have lost their jobs and are unemployed, with an idea for a long term housing project built by the city and operated by formerly homeless residents.

Try this strategy for yourself. Choose one of your challenges and a possible solution. Now select a second, random idea or solution to incorporate. See where it leads you. It may take you down an unexpected path that you've never considered.

While each of these tips can help you generate ideas to respond to specific challenges, there are other things you can do to enhance your creative thinking every day, preparing you to engage your imagination at a moment's notice.

stoking your imagination

TRY SOMETHING NEW EVERY DAY, WEEK AND YEAR

A sure-fire way to shake up your world and jump-start your creativity is to try something new every day, every week and every year. While this may seem daunting, it will become easier as you practice and make it a habit. Begin with the little things – taking a different route to school, listening to a different type of music on your iPod, or wearing a different style of clothing. Then work toward bigger shifts—eat lunch with someone new once a week, watch a documentary show about something you don't know, commit to taking ten minutes to research one topic from the newspaper each week. Finally, reflect on the choices you make each year and determine where you can try something new. Perhaps it will include signing up for an unusual elective class at school, auditioning for the annual musical even though you've never been involved in theatre, or volunteering two hours a week at the local food bank. Stepping into new territory as often as possible will open your thinking, connect you to new people, and stimulate a wealth of new ideas.

MAKE TIME TO PLAY

Think of a child busy at play. They'll spend hours pouring water from a cup into a bowl or stacking wooden blocks in towers. And while they play, their brains are making thousands of connections, learning with each move they make. Playing as a way of learning is something we often neglect doing after early childhood, but it is one of the greatest, most effective ways to stimulate the brain and enhance your thinking skills. Finding ways to play as a teenager can be challenging. However, it is well worth the effort to find ways to play.

Do you enjoy card games, building models, throwing pottery, or acting in plays? List some activities you like to do where you can let your mind (and body) play:

- ______________________________
- ______________________________
- ______________________________
- ______________________________
- ______________________________

READ VORACIOUSLY

Nothing can stimulate the mind, invigorate the senses and open new worlds like reading. It is truly a passport to new worlds. Many of the world's greatest thinkers and artists swear by their voracious reading habits, as it keeps their minds active, expanding their perspectives and experiences with each page. Take a moment to answer the following questions about your reading habits:

- Do you read everyday?
- Do you prefer fiction or nonfiction?
- Do you read across different genres? Which are your favorites?
- Do you read works by authors from different countries, cultures, eras? If so, who?
- Do you read several authors offering a variety of perspectives on one subject?
- Do you read for entertainment?
- Do you read for historical perspective?
- What is the best book you've ever read? Why?
- Which author inspires you the most? Why?
- What is the most imaginative book you've read?
- Can you credit a book for changing your life? If so, which one?
- Do you prefer books to movies? Why or why not?

- What would your life be like without books?
- What would your world be like if you committed more time to reading?
- What is something you'd like to learn more about? What could you read to help you?

TRAVEL

Imagine rowing through the Venetian canals on a gondola, shopping for aromatic spices at a New Delhi market, or eating Dim Sum in a small café on the bustling streets of Shanghai. Nothing opens new worlds and stimulates the imagination like traveling to foreign lands. Unfortunately, we're all not able to travel the world whenever the desire strikes. However, we can experience other cultures by trying new foods, listening to native music, viewing foreign films or reading literature written abroad. If you can't travel with your body, insist on traveling with your mind.

List several places you'd like to travel to:

1. ______________________________
2. ______________________________
3. ______________________________
4. ______________________________
5. ______________________________

What can you do now to experience these places? Be specific – name a restaurant you can go to, a film you can rent, or a person you can meet. Take time to share your responses with classmates. You might be inspired by others' ideas.

DAYDREAM, DOODLE, DANCE OR DAWDLE

Perhaps the most important thing to do to boost your imaginative powers is to take the time to daydream. We live in a culture that rewards productivity. As a result, spending time allowing the mind to wander rarely receives priority. Yet it is critical for stimulating imagination. When we doodle, we let the mind roam; when we dance we shake things up; and when we dawdle we relax—all sure-fire ways to stoke the imagination. We discussed how creative thinking requires "suspending what we know" about a given problem or situation. These steps help us suspend what we know by emptying our minds and shifting our perspectives so that new ideas can emerge.

Stoking the imagination is fun and can seem like child's play, yet it is the key to generating new ideas. Playing allows us to flex the muscle of imagination so that we can unleash innovations that change the world.

MOVERS & SHAKERS

In 1976, Fulbright scholar, Professor Muhammad Yunus, imagined a banking system set up to lend money to the rural poor in Bangladesh. His idea was for families, especially women, to receive small loans, sometimes as small as twenty-five dollars, so that they could create items for sale in the local markets. The proceeds from the sale of these goods helped them improve their means of living while allowing them to pay back the loans.

Nobel Laureate, Muhammad Yunus, founder of the Grameen Bank

The creative financing idea blossomed into what is now known as The Grameen Bank, meaning "bank of the villages." The project was extremely successful, giving birth to the concept of micro-credit (lending small sums of money). The Grameen Bank and micro-credit has become an exemplary model for providing loans to the rural poor throughout the world. Such lending has helped millions of people develop the skills and means for earning a living in some of the most impoverished regions on earth. Together, The Grameen Bank and its founder, Muhammad Yunus, were jointly awarded the Nobel Peace prize in 2006.

Muhammad Yunus is a great example of someone using his imagination to create new institutions that revolutionize the world. However, people can use their imagination to simply shift how they respond to people or problems, thereby changing their own life, and often those around them.

Take a moment to consider a person in your life who "pushes your buttons." Now reflect on how they trigger your frustration or unleash your emotions. Do they say the wrong things at the wrong times, taunt you, or push you to respond in negative ways? Take a moment to imagine other ways of reacting to this person. What might these look like?

Mohandas Gandhi, our great thinker from history profiled in this chapter, changed the world by shifting his responses to outside circumstances.

GREAT THINKERS FROM HISTORY

Mohandas Karamchand Gandhi 1869–1948

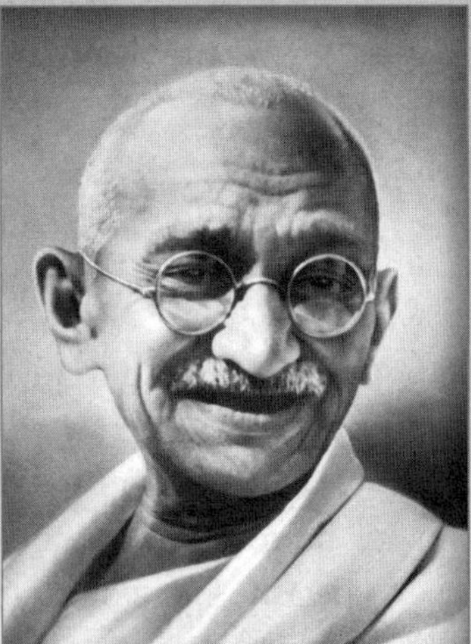

Mohandas Karamchand Gandhi was a leader and great thinker who single-handedly influenced India's strike for political independence from the British. He is perhaps best known for his practice of nonviolence and peaceful resistance. And while these concepts were not new, his use of them as political weapons was revolutionary. Following his leadership, many Indian citizens organized together to boycott foreign made goods and resist British domination in peaceful, yet powerful ways. He also applied his nonviolence tactics to try and alleviate poverty, advance women's rights and help India develop economic self-reliance. His imaginative use of applying peaceful means of civil disobedience impacted not only India, but the entire world.

Aung San Sui Kyi, a pro-democracy activist from Burma, employed Gandhi's tactics of using nonviolence and peaceful resistance for political change. However, at the time of this publication, she is being held under house arrest by the Mynamar government. Ms. Aung San Sui Kyi, the 1991 Nobel Peace Prize winner, is involved with the PeaceJam mission, and is the only Nobel laureate that is imprisoned because of her political activism.

what are you willing to imagine?

John Lennon sang about a world he imagined. If you were asked to add two more verses (each with six short lines) to his song *Imagine*, what would you write? What is your vision for our world in the 21st century? Try your hand at song-writing and let your imagination soar.

Imagine

You may say I'm a dreamer
But I'm not the only one
Someday I hope you'll join us
And the world will live as one

John Lennon . . . and you

POWERFUL QUESTIONS FOR DISCUSSION

1. How can creating a mental image of what you want to write before you begin affect your writing process?

2. How did the world that Martin Luther King, Jr. imagined compare to the world that Ivan Suvanjieff imagined?

3. Why do politicians need creative thinking skills? Why do artists need critical thinking skills?

4. How do metaphors stimulate our imagination?

BUILDING SKILLS
FOR THE TWENTY-FIRST CENTURY

Challenging Your Thinking

CREATING AN IMAGINATION ACTION PLAN

On a scale of 1–10, how imaginative are you (1 is low, 10 is high)?

1	2	3	4	5	6	7	8	9	10

What is the most imaginative thing you've done? What made it so?

When did you use your imagination last week? What pushed you to think creatively?

Describe an event this year that required you to use your imagination. Did you enjoy it?

Do you enjoy creating visions of things in your mind?

How do you play?

How often do you play?

Do you have an activity that you do where you lose yourself, becoming unaware of time passing? Why do you enjoy this activity?

Who is the most imaginative person you know? What makes them this way?

What in your life requires you to think imaginatively?

How could you improve your imagination at school?

What are you willing to do to improve your imagination at home and in your personal life?

List four specific actions you'll commit to doing to improve your imagination:

- *Today*
- *This week*
- *This month*
- *This year*

Share these commitments with fellow classmates. Take time to check in tomorrow, next week and next month to report on what you discover.

Practice What You Learned

YES, AND...

We've discussed several examples where people used their imagination to creatively address difficult issues in the world.

Look around at your own community. Consider your school, your neighborhood, or a place where you spend some of your time. What conflicts exist in these settings? Is racial tension or prejudice prevalent? Are there students who have little access to health care? What are the needs you see as you step out your front door? Take a moment to reflect and write down the issues you observe:

-

- ______________________________
  ____
  ____
- ______________________________
  ____
  ____

Choose one of the issues you listed above. Now create as many different possible solutions as you can by saying "Yes, and..."

Begin by listing one possible solution. Now write "Yes, and ..." and complete the thought with a second solution. Now write the second solution and add "Yes, and..." and generate a third solution. Each solution can build on the previous one. Continue this process until you've generated at least ten solutions to the original problem.

____

yes, and . . . ______________________________

yes, and . . . ______________________________

yes, and . . . ______________________________

yes, and . . . ______________________________

yes, and . . . ______________________________

yes, and . . . ______________________________

yes, and . . . ______________________________

yes, and . . . ______________________________

yes, and . . . ______________________________

yes, and . . . ______________________________

Putting Your Heads Together

SOLVING THE WORLD'S GREATEST PROBLEMS

Finding a way to keep peace across international borders and to combat terrorism is one of the greatest challenges facing the world today.

Who is responsible for keeping the peace? How can terrorists be held accountable for the damage they inflict? Should an international peace keeping organization be charged with such a mission?

Looking at the problem. Choose three other classmates to work with on this project. As a group, research one terrorist activity that has occurred within the last fifty years. Define who the players were, what the issues were, and what resolution, if any, occurred.

Imagining solutions. Now step back and imagine an international peace keeping organization created to fight terrorism. What might this organization look like? How would it operate? Who would pay for the expenses? What authority might the organization have? Who would decide on the rules? Who would enforce them? And finally, how would the organization be governed? As you create your ideal organization, make sure to research what is being currently done to solve these problems. How will your organization reflect what currently exists? How will it differ?

Sharing your solutions. Each team will collaborate on an article to be written and posted on a classroom blog. The article should explain the organization that you and your team have imagined, and discuss how your organization would be implemented and managed.

Evaluating ideas. Each team will then write a collective response to all the other teams' postings, commenting on how they believe the imagined organization will meet or fail to meet the objectives stated above.

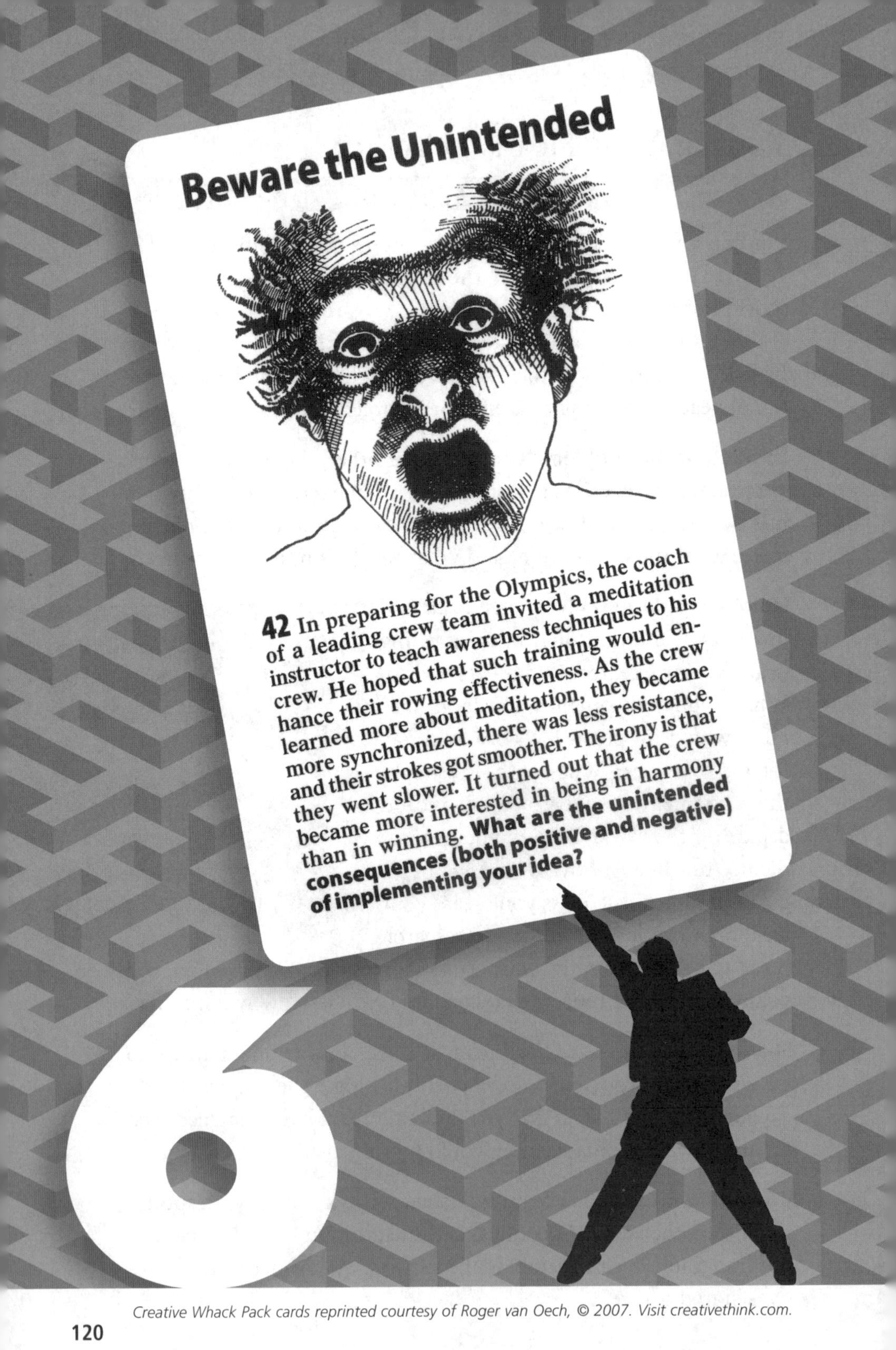

Beware the Unintended
42 In preparing for the Olympics, the coach of a leading crew team invited a meditation instructor to teach awareness techniques to his crew. He hoped that such training would enhance their rowing effectiveness. As the crew learned more about meditation, they became more synchronized, there was less resistance, and their strokes got smoother. The irony is that they went slower. It turned out that the crew became more interested in being in harmony than in winning. **What are the unintended consequences (both positive and negative) of implementing your idea?**
6

Creative Whack Pack cards reprinted courtesy of Roger van Oech, © 2007. Visit creativethink.com.

how to evaluate

Imagine you're facing a problem. You've put your critical and creative thinking skills to work to observe the issue, generate relevant questions, analyze the information you've gathered, and imagine potential solutions. Now it's time to apply the solutions and evaluate the outcomes.

For years you've probably heard math teachers remind you over and over to check your work before turning in your test. Yet how many of you have missed problems on tests that, had you reviewed your work and evaluated your solutions, you would have caught your mistakes?

Evaluating your work is a step that's easy to overlook. Often, we're so happy to finally arrive at a solution, we fail to look back and reflect on what we've done. But making a habit of evaluating your thoughts and actions is essential for effective critical and creative thinking.

In simple terms, to evaluate your outcome you must ask whether your solution, in any given instance, solves the problem. And then you must ask why. This step not only assures that you end up with an appropriate solution, but it opens the door for learning from mistakes when your solutions don't work; and learning from successes when your solutions do work.

The famous inventor, Thomas Edison, mastered this step of evaluation. In fact, his most noted discovery, the light bulb, resulted from evaluating an idea that had been around for 50 years. The idea wasn't actualized until Mr. Edison studied why solutions weren't working, before finally arriving at an idea that did work: placing a carbonized filament

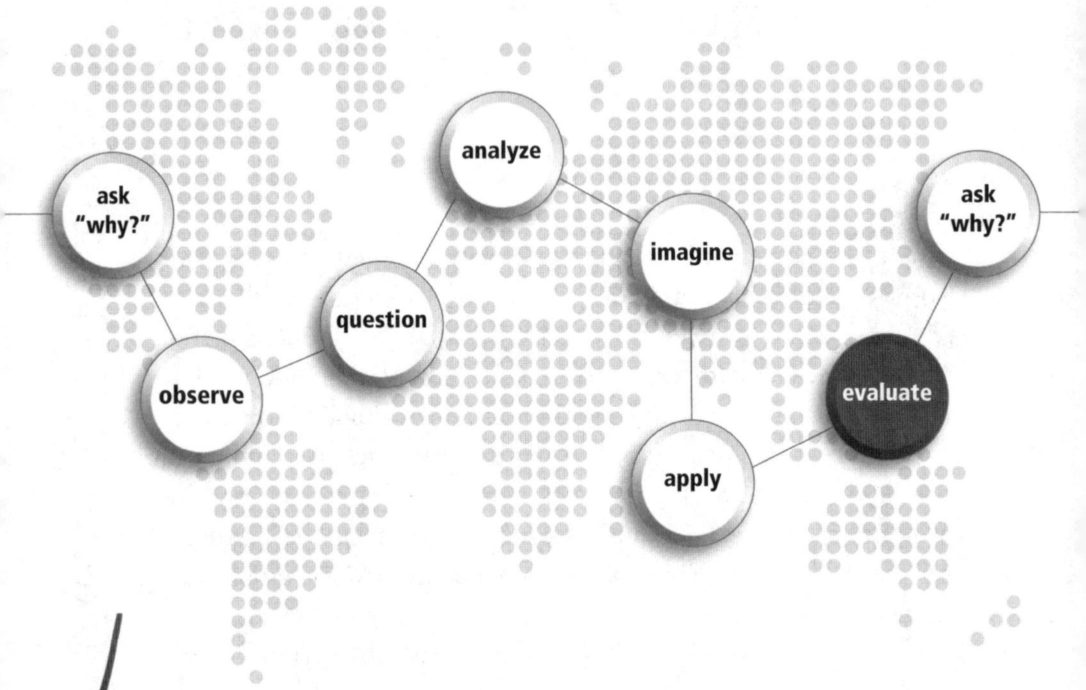

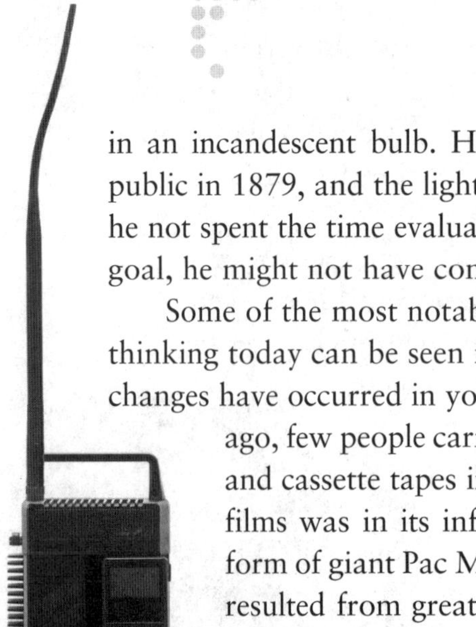

in an incandescent bulb. He introduced the technology to the public in 1879, and the light bulb as we know it was born. Had he not spent the time evaluating solutions that fell short of their goal, he might not have come upon his greatest invention.

Some of the most notable examples of critical and creative thinking today can be seen in the field of technology. Sweeping changes have occurred in your lifetime alone. Only twenty years ago, few people carried cell phones, they listened to CDs and cassette tapes instead of iPods, digital animation in films was in its infancy, and video games came in the form of giant Pac Man machines. All these changes have resulted from great thinkers pushing the boundaries of technology by evaluating what works and what doesn't, and then improving on the ideas. One such thinker, who has magically married technology and creativity, is the famous film director, George Lucas.

GREAT CREATORS OF TODAY

George Lucas, creator of the epic film series, *Star Wars,* and the founder of Industrial Light and Magic, has single-handedly revolutionized the way visual/special effects are created for movies. Born in 1944, Lucas grew up in California, more interested in car racing than academics. A car accident just before he graduated high school changed his life. This tragic event nearly left him dead. Lucas said, "You can't have that kind of experience and not feel that there must be a reason why you're here. I realized I should be spending my time trying to figure out what that reason is and trying to fulfill it." So Lucas spent time improving his grades at a local junior college before attending the University of Southern California's Film School. Afterwards, he became an apprentice at Warner Brothers' Studio and eventually produced several films. His biggest breakthrough came in 1977 when he released the first film in his *Star Wars* series, one of the most successful films of all time. He earned seven academy awards for this effort. Other blockbusters include the *Indiana Jones* series.

Lucas used his expertise to develop technology that enhances the sound and visual effects in film. One of his several companies, Industrial Light and Magic, is known world wide as a premier production facility that incorporates digital technology to produce stunning special effects. ILM has been associated with fourteen films earning Oscar awards for visual effects, and has been awarded seventeen technical achievement awards from the Academy of Motion Picture Arts and Sciences. Mr. Lucas received a medal from President George Bush for his outstanding achievements in technology and film.

Sources: www.ILM.com, www.imdb.com, http://en.wikipedia.org/wiki/george_lucas

George Lucas's successes haven't come easily. They are the result of his testing ideas over and over again, evaluating each step of the production process—from writing the scripts to generating the sound tracks and special effects.

Earlier we talked about evaluating as simply asking whether a solution works or it doesn't. But let's go deeper with this concept. The Webster's II dictionary defines *evaluation* as the process of determining something's value, of examining carefully, or appraising. When we think of evaluating technology we might ask questions such as:

- Does the technology achieve the desired outcome?
- Does the technology produce additional unwanted results?
- Can the technology be duplicated?
- Can the technology be improved?
- Is the technology transferable to other areas?
- Are there other long-term effects caused by the technology?
- What are the short-term effects?
- Is the technology understandable by others?
- Is the technology cost-effective?
- Are there simpler ways to achieve the desired outcome?

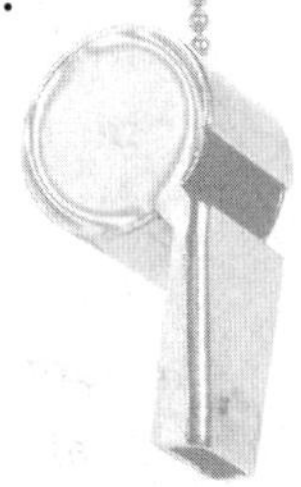

TRYING IT OUT . . .

Practice evaluating these advances in technology by asking the questions listed above and discussing your responses:

The atom bomb

____

____

____

Electric cars

____

____

____

Solar energy

Pesticides

The internet

Concealed weapons

Genetically engineered corn

Any others you'd like to consider . . .

GREAT THINKERS FROM HISTORY

Albert Einstein

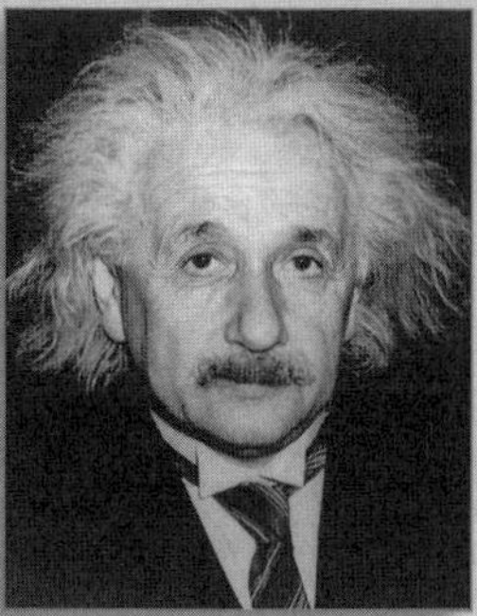

Albert Einstein, the 1921 Nobel Prize winner in physics, was born in 1879. He is considered to have had one of the greatest minds of all time. He was educated to teach physics and mathematics but could not find a job in his field, so he accepted a job as a technical assistant in a Swiss patent office. During the days he'd review patents that had been submitted to the office, identifying why each of them would not work. His assignment was to find the fatal flaw in each idea. While this position was not glamorous, and a step down from what he was trained to do, it gave him the opportunity to develop the critical thinking skills to effectively evaluate ideas.

Had Einstein become a professor right out of school, he may have never fine-tuned these evaluation skills. And it was these skills which ultimately led him to discover shortcomings in Sir Isaac Newton's scientific theories. Einstein's infamous Theory of Relativity directly evolved from his critical evaluation of Newton's law of mechanics, in which he attempted to reconcile the laws of mechanics with the laws of electromagnetic fields. Einstein's work dramatically affected science and the advancement of technology, from the discovery of the Atom bomb to the development of lasers. Einstein once said that his success was directly related to his ability to evaluate ideas that he developed in the Swiss patent office.

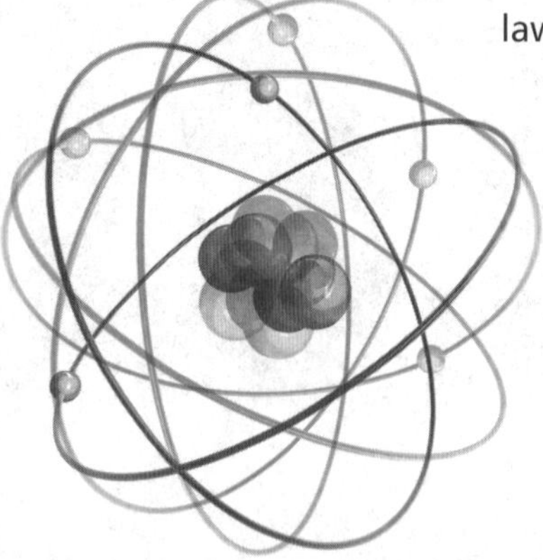

Whether you are inventing technology to change the world, or navigating your day to day life at school, you need to effectively evaluate your actions, abilities and attitudes to position yourself on the best possible path for life after high school.

Imagine going through your classes and never receiving a grade or teacher feedback. It would be difficult to assess if you are doing well and how you can improve without being given this information. As a result, evaluating students is a major responsibility for teachers. But when it comes to your personal life, you often must depend on yourself. And evaluating yourself can be challenging. It requires being open and honest, being willing to consider critical feedback, and being committed to reviewing your choices and actions.

One easy way to evaluate your performance in various areas of your life is to rate it by assigning a number between 1 and 10 (1 being low and 10 being high). This tool offers an opportunity to take a quick look at where you are doing well, where you are okay, and where you can improve.

Try this assessment to practice evaluating the various areas in your life.

evaluation assessment

On a scale of 1–10 (1 being low, 10 being high) rate the following areas of your life.

PERSONAL

_____ I have healthy eating habits.

_____ I get enough sleep each week.

_____ I care for my body by exercising, avoiding drugs/alcohol, etc.

_____ I set tangible short and long term goals.

_____ I'm ambitious and motivated to pursue my dreams.

_____ I take time to reflect on my goals and the manner in which I conduct my life.

Other questions I can ask to evaluate my personal life:

____

____

____

Changes I can make:

____

____

____

ACADEMIC

_____ I take my classes seriously and complete all the required work.

_____ I demonstrate effective study habits.

_____ I take initiative in my learning.

_____ I follow through on academic tasks.

_____ I demonstrate leadership.

_____ I strive to remain curious.

_____ I seek out academic mentors who can help me with my education.

Other questions I can ask to evaluate my academic performance:

____

____

____

____

Changes I can make:

____

____

____

____

FAMILY

_____ I participate in family activities.

_____ I take time to reflect on the role I play within my family.

_____ I demonstrate care and concern for family members.

_____ I invest emotional energy in my family.

_____ I show respect for myself and others in my family.

Other questions I can ask to evaluate my relationship with my family:

____

____

____

Changes I can make:

____

____

____

WORK

_____ I demonstrate a strong work ethic.

_____ I do my best on the job even when tasks seem menial.

_____ I reflect on what I'm doing now and how it might serve me in the future.

_____ I make smart choices with the money I'm earning.

_____ I have financial goals.

_____ Saving money is important to me.

_____ I ask for feedback to improve my performance.

_____ I apply feedback to improve my performance.

_____ I go the extra mile to give more than is expected of me.

Other questions I can ask to evaluate my work performance:

____

____

____

Changes I can make:

____

____

____

SOCIAL

_____ I reach out and connect with others.

_____ My friends and peers inspire me to be my best.

_____ I establish healthy boundaries with my peers.

_____ I surround myself with positive people.

_____ I support my friends.

_____ I'm proud of the role I play in my peer group and community.

Other questions I can ask to evaluate my social life:

____

____

____

Changes I can make:

____

____

____

There are many benefits to evaluating your strengths, weaknesses and areas for improvement in your personal life. Several years ago a student, not much older than you are now, took time to evaluate his and his fellow students' academic and social needs. What he did with this information revolutionized the way young people now network and socialize around the globe.

INNOVATIONS
CHANGING THE WORLD

Mark Zuckerberg evaluated the ways college students interacted—and he saw opportunity. While attending Harvard University, Zuckerberg and several friends developed computer programs that allowed students to interact and learn more about each other. The software also gave students the opportunity to post information about their classes. Zuckerberg's ideas continued to blossom. In February 2004, from their college dorm room, Zuckerberg and his friends launched Facebook, a website that allows people to communicate more efficiently with friends, families and coworkers.

Within months, Facebook was an immediate success at colleges all over the northeastern United States. Zuckerberg assessed the potential of his idea and decided to drop out of Harvard and establish offices in Palo Alto, California. The company is now a worldwide phenomenon with over 150 million active users. Time Magazine recently named Zuckerberg as one of The World's Most Influential People of 2008—not bad for an idea hatched in a college dormitory room!

This revolution in social technology has changed how we communicate and present ourselves to the world. As a result, it is more important than ever to use our critical thinking skills and evaluate how we interact with such technology. While websites such as Facebook and Myspace open many doors, you must be cautious about how you use these networks.

Many of you are familiar with the danger of strangers misrepresenting themselves on such sites. But did you know that what you post about yourself becomes public knowledge for all to see? George Stein, an owner and director of summer camps says he vets all counselor applicants by investigating the information they post on social networking sites. He says he's turned down several potential candidates because of pictures and writings that they never dreamed would land in the hands of someone interviewing them for a job. George Stein is not alone. Many employers today follow the same protocol. So be prudent with what you post about yourself on the internet and evaluate your actions, knowing that a future employer will have access to your photos and comments!

As never before, the advances in technology demand that we evaluate how technology is used to avoid danger and destruction. Technology can be good or bad, depending on its application. Whether you're a teenager navigating social networking sites, or a scientist creating lasers or gas bombs, the evaluation process is imperative for weighing the benefits of technology against its potential destruction.

POWERFUL QUESTIONS FOR DISCUSSION

1. How could the technology that we rely on for communicating in the 21st century become a destructive force?

____

____

____

2. Where have you witnessed technology used for purposes other than what it was originally designed for, and its application benefited humanity? Where have you seen it used for other purposes and it became destructive?

____

____

____

____

____

3. Why do you think evaluation skills are imperative in the 21st century?

____

____

____

____

____

4. When has the failure to evaluate a solution become a problem for society?

____

____

____

____

____

BUILDING SKILLS FOR THE TWENTY-FIRST CENTURY

Challenging Your Thinking

RECRUITING EVALUATIONS

This chapter discusses how you can sharpen your critical and creative thinking skills through evaluation. The self assessment asked you to rate your performance in various areas in your life using a numeric scale. Another effective evaluation tool includes peer/mentor/teacher feedback. Asking people whom you respect to give you honest feedback on your performance can help you evaluate your abilities and actions. This activity asks you to identify people from your life who can play this important role in your self evaluation process.

For each category below, list three potential contacts that you can approach for critical feedback. Choose two of these contacts and ask them to write you an evaluation about your performance. Review the feedback you receive and then create an action plan for how you might incorporate this feedback into your life.

For example, if you are considering your work life, you might ask both your manager and a co-worker to write a few short paragraphs evaluating your work ethic, your ability to get along with co-workers, your ability to deal with the public, your attention to detail and your skills at following through with tasks.

As you prepare for college and the working world, you'll be asked for personal references and letters of recommendation. This activity is a perfect preparation for garnering support and evaluation of the work you do!

ACADEMIC LIFE

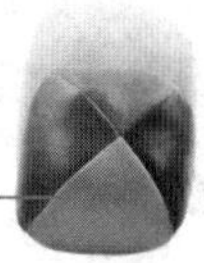

- Three potential evaluators

- Areas to consider for evaluation

WORK LIFE

- Three potential evaluators

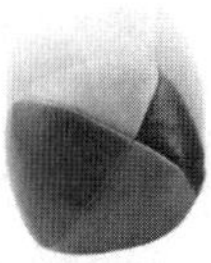

- Areas to consider for evaluation

PERSONAL LIFE

- Three potential evaluators

- Areas to consider for evaluation

Practicing What You've Learned

EVALUATING THE BENEFITS AND RISKS OF STEM CELL RESEARCH

There has been much in the press about the blossoming field of stem cell research. New technologies are shaping the treatment of many diseases. However, some people object to stem cell research. This activity asks you to evaluate the pros and cons of this field.

Find a partner and as a pair research stem cell generation and use.

- Observe what is being done in this field.
- Generate questions about the technology and research these questions for answers.
- Analyze the information you've gathered by comparing, contrasting and connecting ideas to what you already know.
- Consider any assumptions you are making and the perspective that you bring to this topic.
- Imagine the possibilities for this technology.
- Evaluate the implications of stem cell technology. Make sure to consider the questions for assessing technology that are listed in the chapter as you conduct your evaluation.
- Develop your own guidelines for how stem cell research should be conducted.

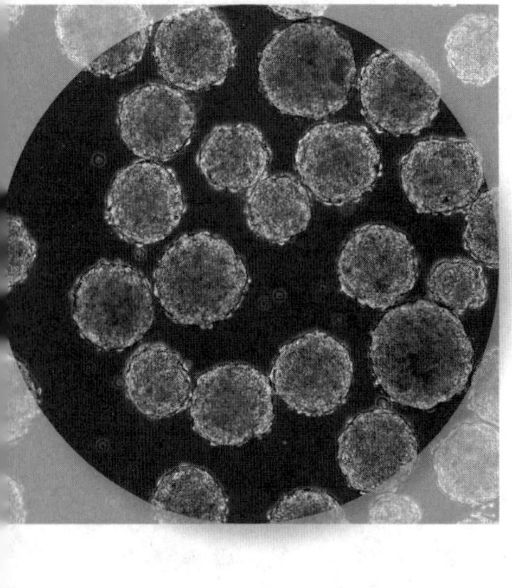

Putting Your Heads Together

SOLVING THE WORLD'S GREATEST PROBLEMS

One of the most debatable issues of the day is how biotechnology can be used responsibly to benefit mankind. At this time, there are no international guidelines to define what is acceptable and what is not regarding biotechnology. And if such guidelines were to ever be instated, how would they be enforced?

To begin this activity, join up in teams of four or five. Start by researching three biotechnology efforts that are underway today. We've already touched on stem cell research and development, but many others are in the works including: animal cloning, genetically engineered food, The Human Genome Project, etc.

- Once you have your three topics, observe the benefits, the costs, the potential for danger, the potential for effective change, etc.
- Now generate a list of questions you can ask about the items on your list to further explore their implications.
- As a team, analyze the information you gathered by comparing, contrasting and connecting the information. Make sure to consider your assumptions and perspective as your reflect on your research.
- Next, determine international guidelines that scientists from around the world should follow and a solution for how you would implement such guidelines. Discuss steps and strategies for enforcing such guidelines.
- Now create an assessment tool for evaluating your solution. What questions should you ask to test your solution against your given goals?
- Finally, create a PowerPoint presentation to present your ideas to the class.

Flex Your Risk Muscle

53 Bull's-eye every time? If so, you're standing too close to the target. If you're not failing every now and again, it's a sign you're not doing anything very innovative. Everyone has a "risk muscle." You keep it in shape by trying new things. If you don't, it atrophies and you're no longer able to take chances. **How can you exercise your risk muscle?**

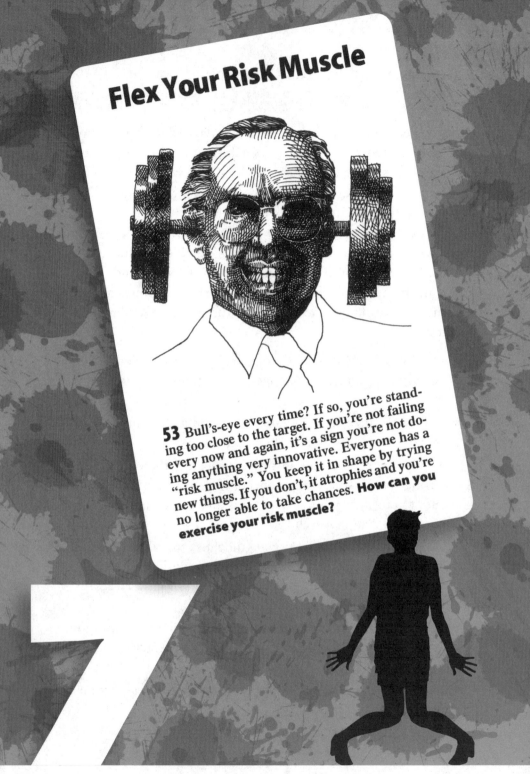

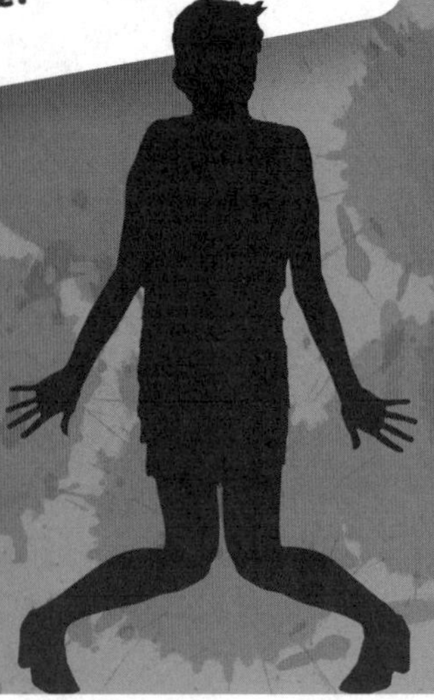

7

Creative Whack Pack cards reprinted courtesy of Roger van Oech, © 2007. Visit creativethink.com.

how to risk

You may wonder what risk has to do with critical and creative thinking. But most problem solving involves some level of risk. At a basic level, any time you choose one solution over another, you risk making the wrong choice. But when you search for the best possible solution to any given problem by trying innovative solutions, you must be prepared to deal with inevitable failures from time to time. For this reason, we've dedicated an entire chapter to this important topic.

We've all heard that failure is the foundation to great success. Although this is true, it is also true that nothing stifles critical and creative thinking like failure. The fear of failing keeps us from trying fresh approaches. It hijacks our deeper level thinking. And it can keep us from honestly evaluating our solutions. For many, it is easier to ignore a failed outcome, than to admit defeat.

The ability to risk and handle failure is at the heart of critical and creative thinking. And as a result, we must learn how to develop these skills. So the purpose of this chapter is to examine how to risk, how to make the best mistakes possible and how to turn these difficult experiences into fuel for success.

Every successful entrepreneur has had to rely on these skills. In fact, risk taking is central to entrepreneurship.

So, we will use it for this chapter's lens. But before we consider world class entrepreneurs, let's look at students like you.

There are students who take endless risks—some good and some bad. They easily venture into new territories, try new things and spend much of their time wrestling with their mistakes. On the other end of the spectrum are students facing opposite challenges. So used to performing to perfection, they avoid putting themselves into situations where they might fail. Taking risks for these students can be daunting.

Where do you fit in the spectrum? Do you take irresponsible risks or are you risk adverse? How willing are you to push your limits to expand your world? Complete the following questions to assess your relationship with risk taking.

risk-taking assessment

HOW WILLING AM I TO MAKE A MISTAKE?

Rate your responses on a scale of 1 to 5 (1 being low or never; 5 being high or always)

_____ My parents have high expectations of me.

_____ I have high expectations for myself.

_____ I'm encouraged at home to try new things, even if it means failing.

_____ My parents take responsible risks and push themselves to learn.

_____ My school encourages me to move out of my comfort zone.

_____ Failing is embarrassing.

_____ I'm curious about new cultures and want to travel extensively.

_____ I reach out and talk to new students.

_____ I keep my shortcomings to myself.

______ I prefer to fail in private rather than in public.

______ Once I fail at something, I'm reluctant to try again.

______ I have a habit of making poor choices.

______ I put myself in danger through risky behavior.

______ I've grown up in a culture where irresponsible risk taking is normal (drinking excessively, driving dangerously, excessive gambling, etc.)

______ I've been hurt by others' irresponsible mistakes.

______ I've benefited from others by learning from their mistakes.

______ I'm fearful of repeating mistakes my parents have made.

Answer each of the following questions with a short response:

What do my answers from above tell me about myself?

What risks do you think your parents wish they'd taken?

What risks do you think your parents regret taking?

What risks do you want to take?

What risks do you want to avoid?

What risks do you regret having taken?

____

____

What is the greatest risk you've ever taken?

____

____

When have you been burned by a risk you've taken?

____

____

Reflect on your responses from above to write a short response about your relationship to risk taking.

My family and culture affect my willingness to take risks by ...

____

____

____

My exposure to negative risk taking is ...

____

____

____

My goals for risk taking are ...

____

____

____

____

We all make both good and bad choices at different times in our lives. But hopefully you'll see that the goal is not to avoid making mistakes. Mistakes happen, no matter how careful and well thought out you are. The important lesson is to evaluate the mistakes and to learn from them. By practicing this you can learn to take positive risks, and create the space for brilliant accidents to happen!

A quick look back in time shows us that many accidents, when looked upon from a different perspective, became the catalyst for great inventions.

accidents happen . . .

POST-IT NOTES

In the 1970s, Dr. Spencer Silver of 3M tried to invent a new type of glue with extreme holding power. His idea flopped. Instead of coming up with something strong, the opposite happened. The adhesive he created was very weak. At the same time his colleague, Art Fry, sang in the church choir and was looking for a bookmark that would allow him to identify pages in the hymnal without damaging the book. He thought about the weak adhesive his friend had come up with, remembering that it was strong enough to stick to surfaces, but could be easily removed, leaving no residue. An idea suddenly surfaced. Fry applied the adhesive on the edges of small slips of paper to make bookmarks for his hymnals, and Post-It Notes, as we now know them, were born.

VELCRO

In the 1940s, a Swiss man named George de Mestral went hiking with his dog. When they returned, he discovered several burrs sticking to both his dog's hair and his own pants. Being curious, he studied the burrs attached to his pants under a microscope. He found that the burrs had small hooks that clung to the smooth fabric of his pants. Instead of picking the burrs off and regarding them as a nuisance, he had an "ah-ha" moment and asked himself, "What if I could design a fastener that had two sides—one with stiff small hooks like a burr, and one with smooth fabric?" He came up with a name for his concept: Velcro—a cross between velour and crochet. As he took his idea to others, many laughed at him. But Mestral persevered. He spent years perfecting his idea and finally patented it in 1955. Today Velcro is a multimillion dollar industry—born from inadvertently brushing up against a bush with burrs.

An extreme closeup of Velcro.

Copyright Robert D. Anderson 2004. http://public.fotki.com/ROBERT1010/scitech/hook_loop_fastener.html

POPSICLES

Some of the greatest inventions don't come from scientific explorations, but from simple mistakes. It was 1905 when eleven year old Frank Epperson accidentally left his soda outside on the porch with a stirring stick in the container. San Francisco was unseasonably cold that evening and the soda froze around the stick. When Epperson found it the next morning, he pulled the frozen soda clinging to the stick from the container and the Popsicle was born. It took eighteen years for Epperson to get a patent for his product, which he named the Epsicle Ice Pop. Years later, his children changed the name to Popsicle and in 1925 the rights to the trademark were sold to Good Humor.

In each of these examples the people didn't set out to invent the product they became known for. Rather, the products resulted from their ability to reshape an accident or mishap. One of the greatest technology applications used today by consumers is Craigslist, the result of what the founder called "a happy accident!"

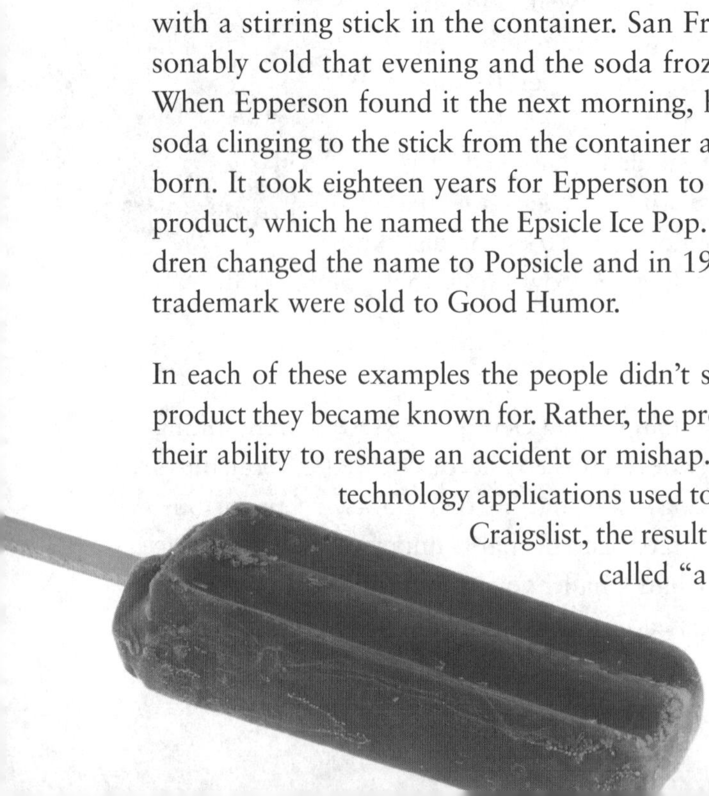

INNOVATIONS
CHANGING THE WORLD

Craigslist, *The Happy Accident*

Craig Newmark, a web-oriented software engineer, was living in San Francisco when he started an e-mail list notifying friends about arts and technology events happening in the city. What began as a living room activity blossomed into one of the ten most visited websites on the internet, and is what Mr. Newmark once referred to as "accidental entrepreneurship!"

Photo credit: Gene X Hwang of Orange Photography in San Francisco, www.orangephotography.com

Newmark's first posting was done in 1995, but his list quickly grew. Without ever planning for it, the list soon included notices of job openings, apartment rentals and sales of goods and services. After a few years, Newmark decided to risk it all and focus on his list full time. His efforts paid off. At the time of this publication the website has a presence in over 450 cities and 50 countries around the world.

What makes Craigslist unique is that it is free to nearly 99% of all its users. The company is built on a culture of trust, helping individuals find jobs, apartments, goods, and services through the network.

Unfortunately, not all mistakes are easy to turn around, nor are all accidents "happy." The reality is that failure hurts. It can be difficult to overcome and can intimidate the best of us.

But as we know, doing something different, whether as an entrepreneur, scientist, artist or ambitious student, requires a tolerance and ability to deal with failure. And yet we live in a world where failure is rarely encouraged. Students are told that taking responsible risks is important, but classrooms are rarely designed to support this action.

As a college student, Maureen, one of the co-authors, had a math professor who gave extremely difficult exams. He believed students entering the field of mathematics must be comfortable with not knowing how to solve the problems. "To advance things in this world," he said, "you'll have to know how to make mistakes and deal with incorrect answers." As a result, he created exams that were nearly impossible to complete. If she was able to answer 50% of the questions correctly, she might have received an A.

Even though she understood where this professor was coming from, it was difficult to change her mindset during his exams. It was much easier to prepare for a test, and to know that if she performed well, she'd be able to answer approximately 95% of the answers correctly and receive an A. Like most students, she'd been conditioned to "succeed" 90–100% of the time.

Perhaps a better model for promoting risk taking is baseball. A batting average over .300 is considered excellent. This means that for every 100 times at bat, the hitter will succeed 30 times, but will fail 70 times. To be successful in baseball, players must be comfortable with approaching the plate, knowing that seven out of ten times they will most likely fail.

How willing are you to make your way through life, knowing you might fail 70% of the time? However, if you approach problems knowing you might make mistakes, the issue then becomes how to make mistakes intelligently!

how to make mistakes intelligently

An intelligent mistake is one that reveals new insights and directions. It is not one that could be avoided by learning from others, planning appropriately and working consciously. Below is a list to help ensure that the mistakes you do make are intelligent ones.

Make your own mistakes. Watch the people around you and learn from their mistakes. If you see things not working well for them, don't try the same tactics. Take a different approach.

Don't fail before you start. Many believe mistakes come from bad ideas. They don't. More often, they result from poor planning. So take time to plan appropriately. Don't rush into action before you've properly prepared.

Don't fail to start. Once you've done the planning, dive in. This is the opposite from the previous point. While preparing is important, don't get stuck in this place. A batter can work to perfect his swing, but he'll never get a hit if he doesn't make it to the plate.

Learn from what others do right. Not only can we learn from others' mistakes, we can learn from their successes. Make a point to consider what works for others and try it for yourself.

Work with the right materials. Working with the right materials goes hand in hand with being prepared. You'll have a hard time painting a masterpiece if your oil paints are dried up and cracked, and it's harder to cook a gourmet meal without fresh ingredients. Do what you can to get the right materials for your work.

Don't do it alone. Make use of the resources around you. Recruit help and support.

Don't rely too much on others. While it's important to have the help and support of others, remember the outcome is ultimately up to you.

Don't deny mistakes. Perhaps the most important step to making mistakes intelligently is to acknowledge, and not deny, the mistake. By denying the mistake, you surrender the opportunity to learn. And this is a key reason why mistakes have the power to abort the greatest of dreams.

It is only natural to want to hide our mistakes, especially the mistakes we make in public. It certainly feels better to smooth over the problem; pretend it never happened and go about our merry way. Yet by doing so, we forego our greatest potential to learn.

Here are three simple rules to facing mistakes:

1. **Don't blame others.** Decipher what you were responsible for and what was out of your control, and then accept responsibility for your role in the mistake.
2. **Find the good in the situation.** You can begin this by asking, "What went well?" Maybe your attempt at starting a school newspaper flopped, but you met a new friend and future collaborator. In the midst of mistakes, many golden opportunities await.
3. **Study what went wrong.** A mistake unexamined, remains just that, a mistake. A mistake examined becomes a blue print for new strategies, new ideas, and new successes. When looking at where things went wrong consider:
   - your set up
   - your execution
   - your follow through
   - your team (if applicable)
   - your unexpected results

TRYING IT OUT . . .

Describe a mistake you've made in the past.

Now analyze the mistake. Did you fail before you started? Did you rely too much on others? Take stock of the situation and see where the problems were.

Describe a mistake you've seen a friend or family member make.

Once again, analyze the mistake. Did they fail to learn from others' mistakes? Did they deny having made a mistake? Take stock of the situation and see where the problems were.

Describe a mistake a business person has made.

Consider where he or she went wrong. Did he do it alone without recruiting support? Did she fail to observe others' successes? Take stock of the situation and see where the problems were.

____

____

____

The following young men have done a brilliant job of analyzing their mistakes, learning what they can from them, and as a result, creating a better life for themselves.

MOVERS & SHAKERS

Bimmer Torres and Ratha Sok, of 2 Kool Productions, LLC, are pictured in the bottom left photo, on the left and right respectively. These young men have joined forces and are applying the lessons they learned from personal mistakes to turn their passion into profitable work.

Ratha Sok spent his teen years in and out of trouble, tagging the streets with graffiti and moving in and out of gangs. "I had a lot of negative habits that were leading to nowhere," he said. While spending time in juvenile detention, he had a life changing experience. He began drawing in exchange for candy and favors, and wondered if one day he might be able to do this for a living. He wrote a letter to the judge, explaining how he planned to use his talents to make money and

improve the community. Once he was released, he returned to high school. At the same time he attended night school and took online classes to make up for the mistakes he made during his previous three years in high school. He became the only member of the school's mural club, seeing it as a leadership opportunity. He committed himself to earning respect in a positive way, with a spray paint can in his hand.

Bimmer, who also shared a passion for graffiti, witnessed Ratha drawing in English class. One day Bimmer showed up at the school on a Saturday to take the ACT test, but it was unexpectedly cancelled. He saw Ratha painting a giant mural on a wall, and joined him, quickly becoming a member of the mural club. Soon after, Sok and Torres decided to join forces and start a company. They named their enterprise 2 Kool Productions, specializing in mural commissions and custom painted hats.

Both Bimmer and Ratha began taking business classes outside of high school to help them launch their company. Yet they've had to learn from mistakes. "We didn't know how much to charge for our time and work. We've had to learn how to better estimate the costs of our supplies and how to invest money in our company so that it can continue to grow." And as it continues to grow, so does their vision. "We'll always want to create beautiful murals that repel vandalism and create unity through art. But now we want to gather people with other talents—dancers, photographers, video artists and others—to work together and build a 2 Kool community."

Today, in addition to running 2 Kool Productions, Bimmer and Ratha host workshops and teach classes to middle and high school students. Their proudest moment: being invited by the City of Denver to create a mural of the then Presidential nominee, Barack Obama, for the 2008 Democratic National Convention.

Our Great Thinker from History for this chapter illustrates how a great idea is only an idea, unless someone has the courage to act upon it. This example shows how one woman took a risk, learned from her mistakes, and overcame the odds to succeed.

Madam C.J. Walker 1867–1919

Madam C.J. Walker (1867–1919) was a pioneering businesswoman, entrepreneur and philanthropist, most noted for the high quality hair care products she invented and sold across the country to African American woman. She is often cited as the first self-made American woman millionaire.

Mrs. Walker was born in Louisiana and was part of the first generation in her family to be born free. Her parents died when she was seven and she lived with siblings until she married, always working a variety of jobs to survive. In her thirties, Madam Walker's hair began falling out. She claimed that an African man appeared in her dreams, giving her an idea for a hair product formula to help people with hair loss. Madam Walker immediately began working on the idea, testing it on her self and friends, working tirelessly to perfect the mishaps and mistakes along the way.

In 1906 she founded Madam C.J. Walker Manufacturing Company to produce and sell her hair products and cosmetics. She created an exceptional marketing and distribution plan, developing a national and international network of Walker sales agents. By 1917 she had the largest business in the US owned by an African American.

Her success didn't come easily. In fact she spent years, traveling across the country selling her products door to door, while simultaneously running a mail order business. "There is no royal, flower-strewn path to success. And if there is, I have not found it. For if I've accomplished anything in life, it is because I have been willing to work hard," she once said.

At the height of her success she employed over 3,000 people, providing opportunities for many to make great livings. As a philanthropist, Madam C.J. Walker was dedicated to sharing her hard earned wealth with important causes including: NAACP's anti-lynching campaign, many schools and orphanages, YMCAs and YWCAs.

POWERFUL QUESTIONS FOR DISCUSSION

1. James Joyce, the world class novelist, wrote that "Mistakes are the portal of discovery." What does this mean to you and how does it apply to your life?

2. What are the risks of being an entrepreneur?

3. Why do you think entrepreneurs must have both creative and critical thinking skills?

4. What is the mistake you are most afraid of making? Why?

BUILDING SKILLS

FOR THE TWENTY-FIRST CENTURY

Challenging Your Thinking

CREATING RISKS

Much of this chapter focuses on learning from mistakes. But you can never learn from mistakes if you don't push yourself to take risks. This activity will ask you to imagine scenarios where you think out of the box, push your own boundaries, risk new ideas and challenge your limits.

Brainstorm responses to the list of *What happens if I . . .*

For example:

If you consider academics, a response might be:

- use trigonometry formulas in my art project

If you consider friendships, a response might be:

- invite two friends from different social groups to join you for a movie

If you consider a summer job, a response might be:

- combine my passion for dogs and economics and create a marketing plan for a doggy hotel to be presented to the neighborhood groomer

Have fun and push yourself to combine even the most random ideas. Take a risk and see what evolves!

What happens if I . . .

What happens if I . . .

What happens if I . . .

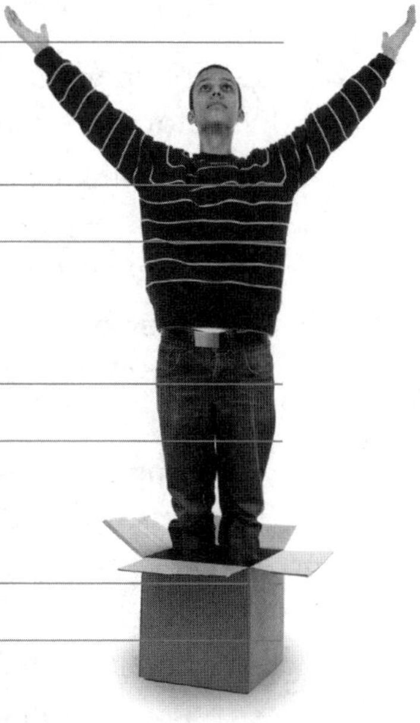

What happens if I . . .

What happens if I . . .

What happens if I . . .

Practicing What You've Learned

ANALYZING GREAT MISTAKES

To begin this activity, join with a partner. Research a start-up business that failed within its first few years of operation. Read all you can about the company (or even better, ask questions if you know the entrepreneurs).

- Observe the factors that contributed to the business's failure (use the list below for guidance).

- Look for any other reasons that might have contributed to the failure.
- Compare this business to other businesses you know. What did they do that worked? What did they fail to do?
- Imagine different approaches that could have been taken to ensure the business's success.

Now pretend you are business consultants making recommendations to the entrepreneur for restarting the company. Role-play this scenario in front of your class.

Seven common mistakes start-up companies make:

1. Not enough money—owners run out of investment money before the company begins generating cash.
2. Not thinking about survival—in the beginning, owners must do all they can to keep their doors open, even if this means doing work that is out of their comfort zone.
3. Losing momentum—it's easy to start with an idea, but harder to keep it going. Everyday owners must work to push their company forward.
4. Doing it alone—the best entrepreneurs know how to build teams with people who have different skill sets than their own.
5. Doing it just for the money—owners who love what they do will have an easier time keeping their momentum and staying committed during the hard times.
6. Not researching whether the idea is viable in a given location or time—sometimes great ideas fall short because of a geographical location or the timing of the start-up.
7. Underestimating the amount of time it takes to get the business going—entrepreneurs need a realistic plan on when to expect the business to generate money, and what they'll do if this timing is not met.

Source: www.powerhomebiz.com, www.youngentrepreneurs.com

Putting Your Heads Together

SOLVING THE WORLD'S GREATEST PROBLEMS

In today's global economy, entrepreneurs and their respective companies are emerging around the world, trading goods and services internationally. In the last few years we've witnessed products on the market that are substandard, some flat out dangerous. We've seen a rise of lead in children's toys, melamine (a plastic by-product) in pet food, cough syrup that kills—mistakes that must be addressed. The rules setting standards for production in the United States don't hold on the international market. So how are we to ensure that the products we're importing to eat, to build with and to rely upon on as a nation, are safe and consumable?

Join up in teams of four or five. Together, research examples where products have caused problems due to a lack of global regulations and standards. Now imagine you are appointed by the president to develop an international regulatory agency that oversees the production and standards of all goods coming in and out of the United States.

Consider the following questions as you develop your proposal:

- What is the purpose of having unified product and liability regulations?
- What would the costs be of launching such a program?
- How would this agency be designed?
- What other agencies have similar missions and responsibilities?
- How would international regulations be implemented?
- Who would monitor international businesses for their compliance to the regulations?
- What would be the consequences for companies producing substandard goods?

As a team, write a collaborative proposal using technology such as a Wiki page or Google Docs to facilitate the group writing process.

Give Yourself A Whack on the Side of the Head

1 The more often you do something in the same way, the more difficult it is to think about doing it in any other way. Break out of this "prison of familiarity" by disrupting your habitual thought patterns. Write a love poem in the middle of the night. Eat ice cream for breakfast. Wear red socks. Visit a junk yard. Work the weekend. Take the slow way home. Sleep on the other side of the bed. Such jolts to your routines will lead to new ideas. **How can you whack your thinking?**

8

Creative Whack Pack cards reprinted courtesy of Roger van Oech, © 2007. Visit creativethink.com.

critical and creative thinking

for school, career, and life

The abilities to observe, question, analyze, imagine and evaluate help you stretch your mind. They shift you into a place of power and opportunity. By regularly exercising these thinking skills, you'll become a strong problem solver for all areas of your life: personal, social, academic and professional.

It won't be long before you are finished with school and ready to join the workforce. When you do, you'll find that many employers look to hire people who can make connections and bring new ideas to the table. In most cases, it's not a specific skill set they are looking for, but rather the ability to think critically and creatively.

Many of the jobs that will be available to you when you enter the workforce full time don't even exist yet. So how are you to learn the skills needed for these jobs while you are a student in high school? Consider that twenty years ago there were no classes teaching web design. However, people who were able to connect what they knew about computer programming and creative design, and apply it to the changing demands and technology, easily moved into this new line of work. So rather than focusing on learning specific job skills for positions that might not be around in twenty years, concentrate on developing the best thinking skills that will help you navigate the changes and trends in the workforce.

This chapter focuses on how the steps for deeper-level thinking apply to you as a student, a future employee and a person preparing to live a rich and full life. The more you practice connecting these thinking skills to the problems you face and decisions you make, the more prepared you'll be to create and maximize opportunities that come your way.

critical and creative thinking for school

ACADEMICS

Connections. You can sail through high school taking classes, passing exams and collecting your diploma by simply doing what each teacher asks of you. Or, you can push beyond the expectations and take charge of your education by strategizing how to maximize your years in high school. Doing this, however, requires deeper thinking. One of the best ways to accomplish this is to observe and question how the learning from one class lends itself to another. How do trigonometry algorithms relate to planets' elliptical orbits in space? How does Russian literature relate to the current rise of the middle class in China? How does the American Revolution relate to Sudan? How does algebra relate to the fall of the Roman Empire? Nothing advances learning more than pushing for connections.

Relevance. *Why do I need to know this?* Have you ever sat in class and asked yourself this question? Good teachers try to make learning relevant for students, helping you see how information relates to your world, why it is important to know, and how you might use it in the future. However, the responsibility to find relevance ultimately lies with you. So how can you make your learning relevant?

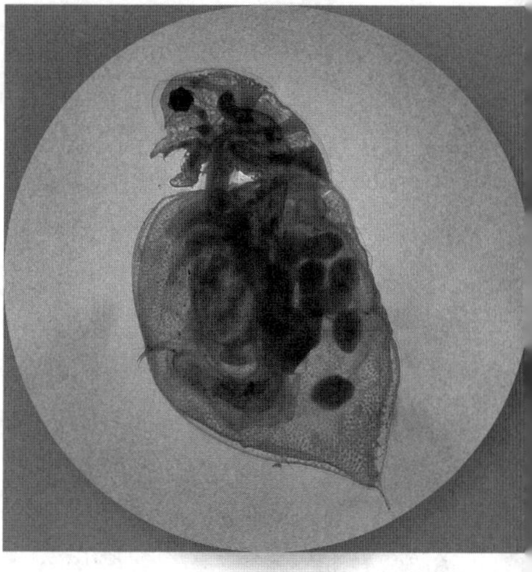

We've just mentioned looking for connections to other learning. You can also challenge yourself to imagine instances where you'd need the specific information. Push your thinking. Pretend you are learning about the life cycles of plankton. Instead of responding with "When will I ever need to know something about plankton?" imagine a career where this information suddenly becomes pertinent. What if you worked for a company developing alternative fuel sources and discovered that plankton can be burned for energy. Suddenly the life cycle of plankton is relevant. Make it a game. Be creative. You'll never know where your mind will take you and it will certainly help imprint the information you're learning in your mind.

Mind conditioning. Students on your school soccer team do sit-ups, not because they improve soccer skills, but because they condition the body. We all know that with finely conditioned bodies, athletes perform at higher levels. Relate this to school. Some of the learning in the classroom can be thought of as mind conditioning. You may never aspire to be a mathematician. But nothing trains your mind to think logically like mathematics, conditioning you for a variety of jobs.

In fact, Maureen, one of the co-authors, minored in mathematics in college but went on to pursue a career in dance choreography. Being able to manipulate sixteen bodies on stage to music with three melodies and complex rhythms was much easier with a mind conditioned by mathematics. So take the time to evaluate how your different classes condition your thinking. You'll never know when it might help you.

extracurricular activities

These thinking strategies aren't limited to the classroom. Apply them to your after school activities as well. While sports and clubs provide opportunities to have fun, explore passions, and develop leadership, they also provide opportunities to enhance thinking.

Make an effort to observe yourself within the context of a team or group. Take time to observe others as well. What do you like about their behavior? What troubles you about your own? Question why and how things are done within your group and challenge yourself to imagine new possibilities. What if your band could raise enough money to travel to Turkey? What if your cross country team collaborated with your swimming team to host a biathlon to raise funds for a charity? Analyze what works for your group and what doesn't. Is there a leadership opportunity for you to claim as you imagine new ideas for your success? Taking the time to evaluate your participation in different activities will not only enhance your thinking skills but will provide you with tools for maximizing opportunities throughout life.

internships, exchanges and other alternative programs

You can also apply these critical and creative thinking strategies to link your education to the outside world. Look to see how you can enhance what you are learning in the classroom with opportunities beyond the walls of your high school building. Imagine you see a future in politics. What if you were able to tie in the curriculum from your civics class with a summer internship working with your state legislator, where you research initiatives and receive class credit for your time?

As the authors of this book, we were privileged to meet a student who wanted to study in Spain his junior year, but his high school didn't have an exchange program. Thinking out of the box, this young man researched other high schools across the country that offered such programs. After having found one from a different state, he petitioned his own school and received permission to enroll in the other school so that he could participate in the exchange program and study for a year in Madrid. With a little creativity, initiative and savvy, you can use your thinking to create amazing opportunities for learning.

MOVERS & SHAKERS

"Service above Self"

Service above Self is the motto for more than 200,000 youth involved with Interact, Rotary's service club for teens. Together, they create incredible learning opportunities while helping those in need. Currently, there are 10,700 Interact Clubs across the world. These clubs are self-governed and self-supported with a mission to serve others. Students from a school can partner with a Rotary Club to set up their own Interact Club, or they can partner with other schools to establish a club.

The goals for participants are to:

- Develop leadership skills and personal integrity
- Demonstrate helpfulness and respect for others
- Understand the value of individual responsibility and hard work
- Advance international understanding and good will

Clubs are encouraged to complete two community service projects a year, with one aimed at furthering international understanding and good will. Here are two examples of projects taken on by club members.

The Interact Club of Keene High School in New Hampshire raised money to help survivors of the 2001 earthquake in El Salvador. Twenty five students traveled with a 43-foot container full of relief items including: $40,000 worth of medical supplies, mattresses, bedding, clothes, toys and sewing machines. During their time in El Salvador, these students helped demolish several irreparable buildings, rebuild four houses, and paint three others. They also helped install five solar-powered water purification systems in villages with contaminated water. These young people exemplify the power of working together to help those in need.

Fifty Interactors from Japan raised money to buy hearing aids for students at a school for the deaf in Thailand. Together, they traveled with their gifts to the school. While there, they visited the poor neighborhoods, helping with building and domestic chores.

TAKE A MOMENT TO REFLECT . . .

How can you think differently about your academic studies? What opportunities are you overlooking?

What are the most valuable skills you are learning from extracurricular activities? How will these skills make you a better thinker? How will they enhance your ability to problem solve?

If you and a few other students started an Interact Club at your school, what international projects would you like to explore? What might you learn from them?

critical and creative thinking for career

Your generation faces a rapidly changing working environment. These days it is rare for someone to enter a job and stay with the same company throughout his or her career. Most people not only change companies, but change careers at some point in their professional life. And you'll be competing for jobs with some of the best and brightest workers from around the globe. Being able to strategize and position yourself in the best way possible throughout your career requires well-developed creative and critical thinking skills.

MAKING CONNECTIONS

Perhaps one of the most important critical thinking skills you'll apply to your career is the ability to analyze and connect what you know with new information. Employees who succeed at making connections with people, ideas and situations, often see themselves getting promoted and moving into the exciting jobs. Whether you're a scientist, salesperson or educator, the ability to connect is critical.

Connecting to people

Have you ever heard the expression, "It's not what you know, but who you know?" While this isn't entirely true, there is some merit to it. Being connected to people opens doors for you. Once the door is opened however, you'll have to demonstrate what you know. But oftentimes, getting the door opened is the crucial step that makes the difference.

So how do you make connections with people? How do you build networks that will aid you in the working world? It helps if you are outgoing. But quieter, more introverted people can excel in making connections as well. Success depends on your ability to think over your goals and make concerted efforts to meet the right people.

Making connections might involve joining a specific club, or asking someone to mentor you. It could involve interviewing a professional in your field of interest or volunteering for an organization. Never underestimate the power of giving time and energy to a cause. Some of the best connections with people are made when you do something for someone else.

Describe a time when your connections to people created an opportunity for you.

___

___

___

Connecting ideas

We've talked about how connecting ideas can expand your knowledge and bolster your creativity. Having a knack for thinking this way will be a huge asset for your career. Blessed are the workers who can envision solutions that solve more than one problem at a time. A great example of this comes from Van Jones, the author of *The Green Collar Economy: How One Solution Can Fix Our Two Biggest Problems*. In this book, Mr. Jones asserts that by the government investing in projects such as installing solar panels, harnessing wind power and building hybrid engines, new jobs will be created for poorer workers, thereby reducing pollution and poverty at once.

What ideas can you connect to address multiple problems?

___

___

___

Connecting situations

Imagine two lawyers starting practices on their own right out of law school. By connecting their situations, they could rent office space together, share a copying machine and split the expenses of a paralegal aide. Knowing how to make connections, and share resources and ideas, is crucial in the working world. Co-ops—commercial enterprises run for the benefits of their owners—were born from this idea. Now it's common to see co-ops for housing, food production, and babysitting. Many smaller arts organizations do cooperative advertising where they publicize everyone's events together under one marketing campaign. Travel agents often bundle air flights, hotels and dinner packages, as a way to connect what they individually offer to potential clients.

Describe two situations that could be connected and ultimately benefit all involved.

____

____

____

developing transferable skills

Because the workforce is constantly changing, thinking about how you can develop transferable skills that apply to a variety of occupations is essential. When Maureen, one of the co-authors of this book, was winding down her career as a professional dancer, she went on a job interview to sell specialized high tech equipment. On the surface, her experiences as a dancer hardly mirrored the qualifications posted for this new position. So she spent time preparing how she'd demonstrate that the skills she'd acquired over the years in dance would transfer to this new field.

She was able to show the employer that her years spent auditioning in front of strangers was similar to cold-calling potential buyers. She was also able to convince him that the discipline she'd developed as an independent artist was something she'd rely on as she set out to self-manage a sales career. And ultimately, she showed that her experience with rejection (a hard reality in the life of a professional dancer) had given her the thick skin she'd need in sales. In the end, she was offered the job over several well-qualified, professional salespeople, all because she persuasively argued the value of her transferable skills.

While developing the necessary critical thinking for your career, take special note of the following three areas: communication skills, managerial skills, and interpersonal skills.

COMMUNICATION SKILLS

Regardless of the career you pursue, being able to communicate effectively will always be important. So how can you think about communication? Begin by observing how you communicate: Do you easily grab people's attention? Do you feel comfortable talking in front of others? Are you able to express yourself on paper? Do you have a strong command of grammar and punctuation? If you answer "no" to any of these questions, consider what you can do to improve your communication skills. Perhaps a year on the speech team will help you overcome stage fright, or two months with a tutor might help you master some basic writing skills.

Once you feel confident in how you communicate, reflect on "what" you communicate. Consider the acronym AAE—audience, assumptions and evaluations. Whenever you prepare to communicate, whether through a paper, letter, phone call or speech, take a moment to think before you begin, and ask yourself these questions: Who is my audience? What assumptions should I make or avoid making about my audience? How will I evaluate my communication? Once you've delivered your message, don't forget to assess its effectiveness. Did your message reach the intended recipients? Did you get the response you were looking for? Did the communication clarify things or make matters more confusing? By taking time to think about how you communicate, you'll be more effective throughout your career.

When have you failed to think about how you communicated? How did it affect you?

____

____

____

____

MANAGERIAL SKILLS

Knowing how to manage others is a vital and marketable skill, and one for you to think about now and begin to develop as a student. Some of the abilities good managers possess are:

- Leading by example
- Dealing with conflict
- Motivating others
- Working as a team player
- Holding others accountable
- Holding yourself accountable

Take a moment to think about this list. Observe which abilities come naturally to you. Which are more difficult?

When in your life have you demonstrated these abilities? When have you wished you were more capable in one of these areas?

The questions below give you the opportunity to reflect on your past and analyze these experiences so that you can connect them to dreams for your future (these can include dreams of future careers, personal relationships, etc.)

A time in my life where I led by example was

___

In the future, I hope to lead by example when

___

A conflict I dealt effectively with was

___

In the future, I'll need to deal with conflicts when

___

I've motivated others when

___

In the future, I'll need to motivate others when

___

The greatest challenges I have being a team player are

___

In the future, I'll need to work with others when I

___

I successfully held someone accountable when I

___

In the future, I'll need to hold others accountable when

___

The managerial abilities you're cultivating now, whether as class president or secretary of the chess club, will serve you in your career. So take advantage of the leadership opportunities available to you, as these skills will help you launch your career.

INTERPERSONAL SKILLS

Last of all, taking time to assess how you relate to others is an important part of applying critical thinking to your career. In general, successful employees have effective interpersonal skills which include proper etiquette, the ability to read others' body language and nonverbal cues, an understanding of how to perform on a team, and a sense of basic political correctness. Competency in each of these areas grows as you mature, but reflecting on what these components mean and what the expectations are in each of these areas will prepare you for the world of work.

When you begin a job, knowing how to properly address your manager, answer the telephones and dress appropriately, all fall under the etiquette category. Taking the time to observe what is expected and appropriate in your given work situation can set you apart from fellow workers.

Successful employees also know how to read people's body language. They can pick up on non-verbal cues, understanding when they might need to back off of an idea, shift tactics, or simply keep their thoughts to themselves. When employees don't have a sense of how their behavior affects others around them, it can be a drain for the entire team.

As the global economy expands, the workforce will continue to grow in diversity. Having a basic awareness of other cultures and practices is imperative. And monitoring your behavior so that your words and actions are not offensive to others is critical for success in the workplace.

Describe a scene from a TV show or movie where a character's lack of interpersonal skills had adverse effects.

THINKING ON THE CUTTING EDGE

Bill Shore, *Founder of Share Our Strength®*

In 1984 Bill Shore used his critical and creative thinking skills to combine two seemingly incongruent ideas about work and career—creating wealth and serving the public interest. In connecting these two ideas, he built a model of "creating wealth to serve the public." And he successfully launched his career from this concept, founding Share Our Strength®, an organization that has generated over $245 million to date in order to support more than 1,000 of the most effective hunger relief organizations around the world.

Mr. Shore acknowledged that charity alone can't solve our world's problems. He saw that new opportunities for generating wealth existed, and could be tapped into in order to help relieve the burden on nonprofits. So he approached chefs, artists, writers and others to do what they do best, and create assets that could then be leveraged to fund anti-hunger activities. Share Our Strength's Taste of the Nation® was modeled after this idea. Taste of the Nation is the nation's premier culinary benefit dedicated to making sure no kid in America grows up hungry. Each spring, the nation's hottest chefs and mixologists donate their time, talent and passion at more than 45 events across the United States and Canada, with one goal in mind: to

SHARE OUR STRENGTH®
NO KID HUNGRY

raise the critical funds needed to end childhood hunger. With support from national and local sponsors, as well as thousands of volunteers, 100 percent of ticket sales from these events support Share Our Strength's® work to end child hunger in America.

See Share Our Strength's® website for additional creative ventures for generating wealth to serve the public at www.strength.org.

critical and creative thinking for life

As you move through school and into the workforce, you'll experience more demands placed on your time. Balancing such demands—paying the bills, getting exercise, raising a family, advancing your career, and caring for your health—can be extremely difficult. Being able to think creatively and critically about how you structure your life can help you handle such challenges.

It is easy to get caught up in the frantic pace of living and neglect thinking about your life. But there is no more important area for you to stop and ask what the consequences will be by not observing, questioning, analyzing, imagining and evaluating your actions. Applying deeper thinking to your life can shift you from a place of simply accepting what happens to you, to a place of power where you can begin making decisions to positively affect your health and well-being.

HEALTH

Unfortunately, health is one of those things that we often fail to appreciate until we no longer have it. But by thinking about the choices you're making regarding how you eat, the amount of sleep you get, your choices around drugs, alcohol and tobacco, and the time you spend exercising your body, you'll be able to affect how you feel in the moment, as well as how you'll feel years from now. Think about the patterns you've established.

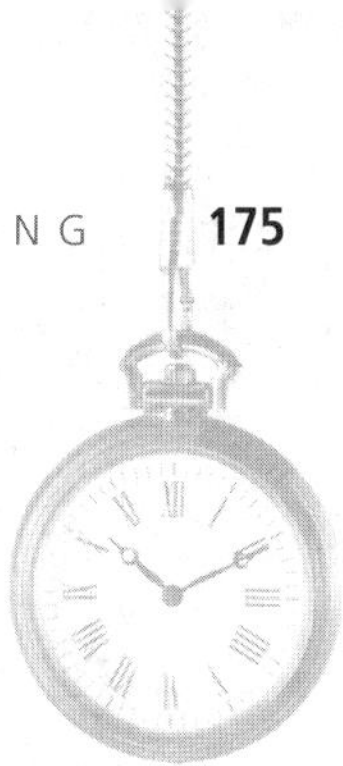

Take a moment to reflect . . .

How are your habits serving or failing to serve you?

How can thinking about your health set you on a path to better living?

What habits do you observe others having that you'd like to establish for yourself?

Analyze the worst habits you have. What are they costing you? How can you rethink these habits?

FINANCES

Another topic that can be a source of great stress for many is finances. Areas to reflect on include: earning money, spending habits, savings plans, and debt. Teenagers often have access to credit cards before they have earning power to pay for their debt. And once you are caught in this vicious cycle, it's hard to get out. Begin by asking what are your financial goals? Do you plan to go to college? Do you hope to one day own your own home? Do you have dreams of traveling around the world? By observing your spending habits

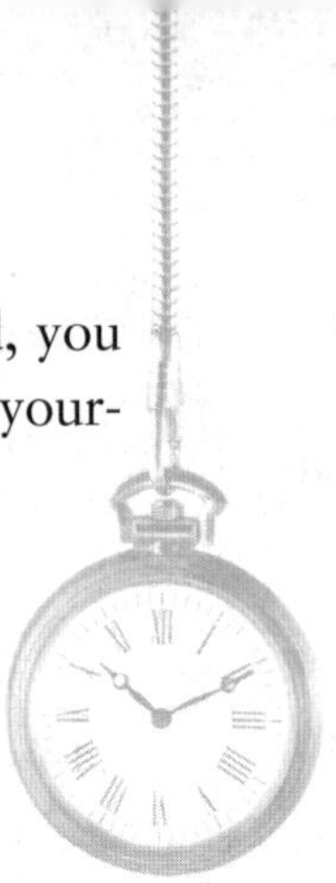

and analyzing the money you earn vs. the money you spend, you can establish a fruitful relationship with money and position yourself to reach your goals.

Take a moment to reflect . . .

What are your thoughts about money (it's hard to come by, there's never enough, etc)?

____

____

Analyze how you spend your money.

____

____

Evaluate the money you earn compared to the money you spend.

____

____

What plans do you have for saving money?

____

____

Do you have a financial mentor or role model?

____

____

RELATIONSHIPS & COMMUNITY

When thinking about how to create the best life possible for yourself, considering your relationships is paramount. It all boils down to whom you care for and who cares for you. These relationships traverse families, friends, boyfriends and girlfriends, workmates and neighbors. Many psychologists agree that as social animals, humans' well-being often directly corresponds to the quality of their relationships. So it is an area in your life certainly worth considering.

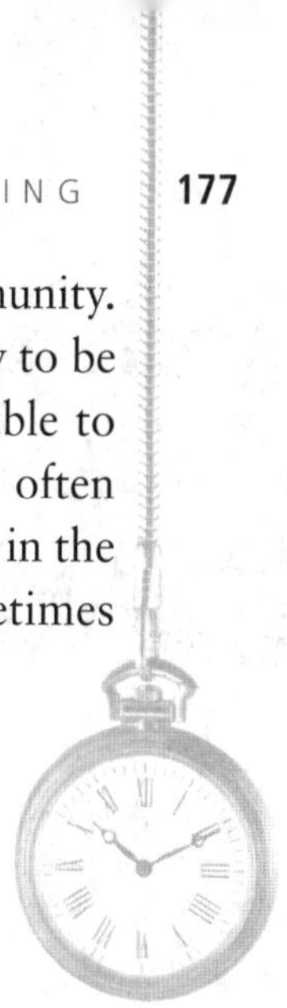

Take time to reflect on how you relate to your community. As life becomes more stressful, finding the time and energy to be involved in your community can be difficult. Yet being able to give and be a part of something bigger than yourself is often essential for well being. And the relationships you develop in the process can be life altering. As the old saying goes, sometimes helping others is the best way to help ourselves.

Take a moment to reflect . . .

Describe your best relationships (family, school, place of employment, neighborhood, etc).

Describe your most challenging relationships.

How are these two similar? How do they differ?

What do your communities offer you (school, neighborhood, teams, work, etc)?

How can you give back to those in your communities?

How can deeper thinking about your role in your communities affect your well being?

Randy Pausch, 10/23/1960–7/25/2008

The Last Lecture

Randy Pausch believed in childhood dreams, enabling others to fulfill their dreams, and having fun along the way. As professor at Carnegie Mellon University, he delivered his last lecture to his work community, as part of a series for professors to offer their words of wisdom as if it were their last time to speak before students. And for Pausch it had real meaning, having just been diagnosed with pancreatic cancer and told he only had months to live.

His lecture has been viewed by millions (a much larger audience than he'd ever intended) and was put into book form by Pausch and his colleague, Jeffrey Zaslow. The book unexpectedly landed on the New York Times bestseller list. But Pausch insisted he did the lecture for one reason only: to pass along a lifetime of advice to his three children, then 6, 4, and almost 2. He never sought the attention he ended up receiving.

The Last Lecture was not about his battle with cancer, and not totally about achieving his childhood dreams—experiencing zero gravity, winning giant stuffed animals, writing for the World Book Encyclopedia, and working for Walt Disney Company—but about how to live a life. "If you lead it in the right way," he says, "karma will take care of itself. Dreams will come true."

His concepts are simple:

- Never lose your childlike wonder
- Have specific dreams
- Get feedback and listen to it
- Don't complain
- Show gratitude
- Be prepared and work hard

Speaking about obstacles, he said, "Brick walls are there for a reason—not to keep us out but to show us how badly we want things." Randy Pausch's simple but profound words remind us of the power we have to create a life in the midst of difficult circumstances. To learn more about Mr. Pausch, you can read his book *The Last Lecture*, or visit his website www.TheLastLecture.com.

Sources: www.NYTimes.com/2008/04/08/Health, www.TheLastLecture.com

As you travel through life, it's certain that, like Randy Pausch, you too will face trials and tribulations—some you can control and some you cannot. And yet it is in the context of these most difficult tribulations that critical and creative thinking can best serve you. When you are up against insurmountable obstacles, your deeper thinking may not change the problem, but it can shape your reactions and responses to the problem. And this is where your greatest creative power lies.

> "An artist takes ingredients that may seem incompatible, and organizes them into a whole that is not only workable, but finally pleasing and true, even beautiful. As you get up in the morning, as you make decisions, as you spend money, make friends, make commitments, you are creating a piece of art called your life."
>
> —*Mary Catherine Bateson from* Composing a Life

POWERFUL QUESTIONS FOR DISCUSSION

1. How are you consciously creating your life?

2. In which areas of your life do you feel that you lack the power to create?

3. How do you condition your mind?

4. Do you think of work as a way to make money, a way to express who you are, or both?

5. How do you see your work in life reflecting who you are as a person?

BUILDING SKILLS FOR THE TWENTY-FIRST CENTURY

Challenging Your Thinking

HOW TO MAKE CRITICAL AND CREATIVE THINKING A HABIT

Now that you've seen how you can apply critical and creative thinking to school, career and life, take time to consider how you can make this deeper thinking a habit. One that you can rely on, that your mind instinctively turns to, as you make decisions throughout your life.

Perhaps the most important step to formalizing this thinking behavior into habit is to carve out time for reflection. Einstein became a master evaluator because he spent eight hours a day at the Swiss patent desk, looking for the fatal flaws in all the patents submitted. Leonardo da Vinci became a master observer because he committed to long hours of solitude where he'd list every observation he could about a given situation.

What can you do to create the time and space in your life to make this type of thinking a habit? Keeping a journal and committing to writing regularly can be an effective tool for thinking. Filling the pages with questions, observations and analysis is a great way to reflect and process decisions you need to make.

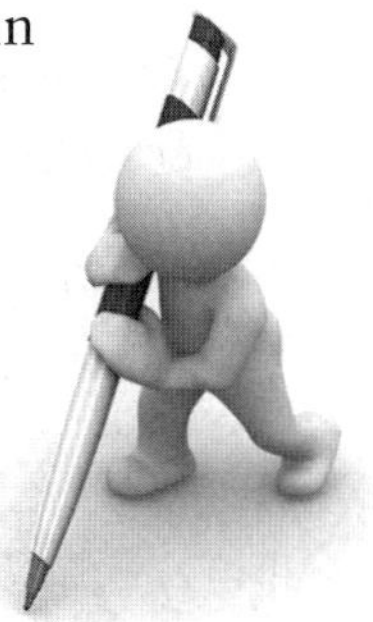

Julia Cameron, in her book *The Artist's Way*, encourages people to take an "artist's date," every week. This date simply consists of going out alone, one time a week, and doing something where you consciously take time to observe. One week you might walk along a stream, another week attend an exhibit at an art museum, or take a camera into the city and shoot pictures of different scenes. The objective is to stimulate your senses, carve precious time for yourself alone, and create a ritual for opening your mind.

The famous choreographer Twyla Tharp, writes about establishing rituals to foster creativity in her book *The Creative Habit*. She says that while most of us think that creativity is made of "ah-ha" moments when the light bulb suddenly switches on in our minds, it's more often the result of dedicated and disciplined work, set in motion by rituals to foster and condition the creative mind. Her ritual: getting out of bed at 5:30 and hailing a taxi to the gym for a two hour workout so that her body, and more importantly her mind, is warmed up and ready for a day of creating dance in the studio.

List habits, routines and rituals you can explore to ensure your commitment to critical and creative thinking. They can be as simple as trying something new everyday. Choose three from your list and commit to them for a month. Keep tabs on how they affect your abilities to make choices in your life, create new ideas for problem solving, and generate a feeling of well being for you.

HABITS, ROUTINES AND RITUALS

Committing to critical and creative thinking in life. Make sure to consider different areas in your life: school, work, family, etc.

HABITS FOR REFLECTION

ROUTINES FOR OBSERVATION

RITUALS FOR CREATIVITY

____

____

____

Practicing What You've Learned

THINKING ABOUT DISCIPLINE

Where do you need more discipline in your life—your study habits, your sleeping routine, regular exercise? Perhaps you're a great student with diligent personal habits. If so, do you need discipline to ensure time for social activities, for fun, for relaxation?

Below is a thinking map. At the top of the following page, list an area in your life that lacks discipline. Then follow through the thinking process, writing down your thoughts through each stage. Finally draft an action plan for creating more discipline in your life in your chosen area.

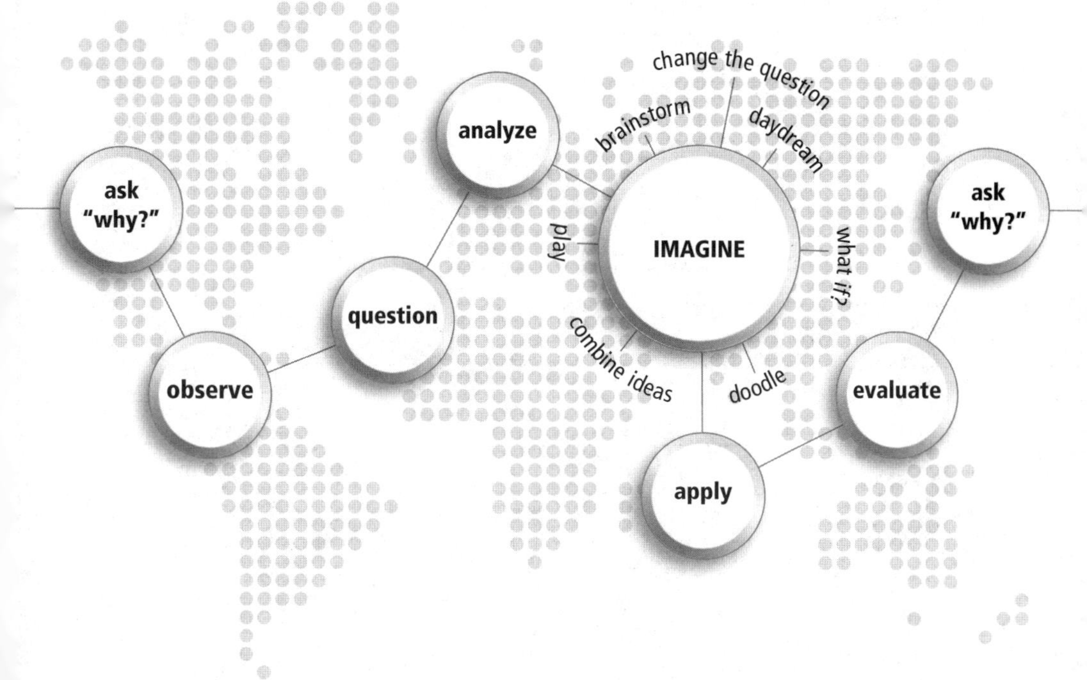

GOAL:

ask "why?"

observe

question

analyze

imagine

apply

evaluate

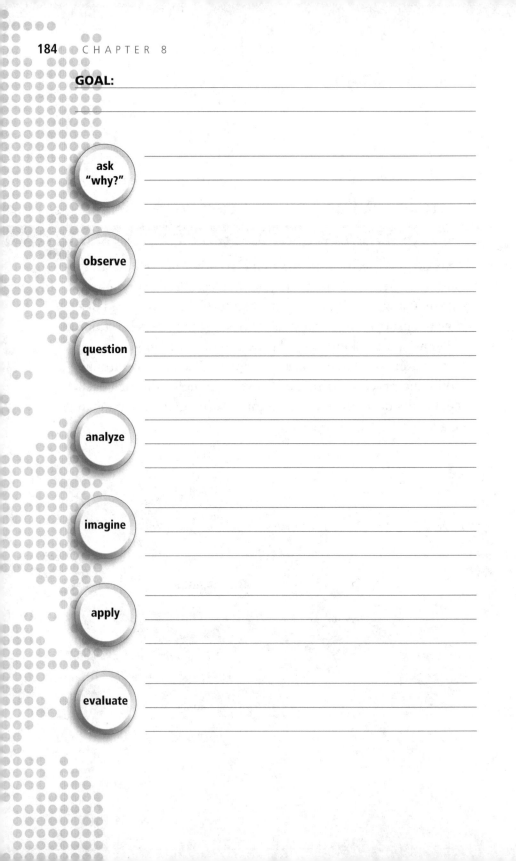

Exchange action plans with a fellow classmate or friend. Check in with each other in a month to see how your plan is working and evaluate whether it needs tweaking. Oftentimes, holding yourself accountable to another person helps you follow through with your commitments.

Putting Your Heads Together

SOLVING THE WORLD'S GREATEST PROBLEMS

The lens for this chapter is work, and to be best prepared for work, young people need education, whether it's in the realm of practical, vocational or analytical skills. Yet many children throughout the world have no access to education. Their exposure to books is limited, and the demands on their time and lifestyle make formal education nearly impossible.

Jean-Francois Rischard, the former World Bank's Vice President for Europe, believes that providing education for all children is one of the greatest challenges facing the world today. This activity gives you an opportunity to consider this challenge and explore some of the possibilities and difficulties in tackling it.

To begin, join in teams of four. Together research and choose a country from the third world that does not have a formal education system in place.

As a team, think through the steps we've covered in this book and record your thoughts and information gathered:

Ask "Why?". What are the costs of ignoring this challenge of providing education for the population you are researching?

Question. Generate questions about the population, economics, political landscape, and cultural beliefs that might influence education policy in your chosen country.

Observe. How are basic lessons of survival taught in your chosen country? What other attempts at education have taken place? Take note of the financial resources and limitations. Observe and record all you can.

Analyze. Study the information you've gathered. What are the causes contributing to the lack of an educational system? How does this population differ from other countries? How is it similar? What patterns have repeated in the country's history?

Imagine the possibilities. What would education for all look like in your chosen country? What systems would need to be put in place? What changes could result? What resources need to be tapped? What leadership needs to be developed?

Evaluate. How would you evaluate your plan? Why would it be successful? What limits will it face? How would you define success?

Apply. Since you aren't in a position to actually apply your plan, use this step of the process to share your plans with the class by creating a short video where you discuss your ideas for implementing an education plan for your chosen country.